SYSTEMIZE YOUR RE
THROUGH DIGITAL AUTOMATION

MW00619236

Exposing the
eLearning Mystery
Secrets to Digitizing Your Business

You ARE AWESOME!!!

Dr Theresa Ashby

THERESA ASHBY, PHD, MBA AND LAURA NEUBAUER

INDIE BOOKS
INTERNATIONAL

ISBN-13: 978-1-957651-35-4
Library of Congress Control Number: 2023904974

Designed by Steven Plummer Design

INDIE BOOKS INTERNATIONAL®, INC.
2511 WOODLANDS WAY
OCEANSIDE, CA 92054
www.indiebooksintl.com

We dedicate this book to the colleagues we have worked with over the many years of our careers. To the mentors and coaches who challenged us and guided us through our entrepreneurial journey. A special thanks to our clients who trusted us to help them scale their businesses by producing digital products and automating their business systems.

A special thank you goes to our families, who have stuck with us through all our endeavors. They continue to trust and support us during trials and tribulations and generously celebrate with us.

Our colleagues, mentors, coaches, clients, and family members have informed and shaped our lives. They have given us the courage and strength to build a business that aligns with our lifestyles.

Contents

Build a business by adding digital products and automation so you can enjoy more freedom, more revenue and create a lifestyle that lets you enjoy your life!

Introduction

Life is either a daring adventure or nothing.
HELEN KELLER

As ENTREPRENEURS, WE find ourselves seduced into believing we will be financially successful and have the time and freedom to be with our family and friends. We learn that we need to work with people one-to-one and in-person because it is the right way to do business. We work hard and max out every hour of every day and are sure to under-promise and over-deliver. We expose ourselves to burnout and frustration—all for a limited amount of revenue, no freedom, and no time. The truth is that today anyone with even a little understanding of technology can surpass what they generate in revenue from a one-to-one business model. Best of all, you can do it without working twelve-hour days. The forty-, fifty-, and sixty-hour workweek is unnecessary with automated work systems. Working from more than one location is an option. The 8:00 a.m. to 5:00 p.m. workday is obsolete.

You don't have to go broke to make money. You don't need to put yourself in debt to start and even grow your business. In this book, we share step-by-step secrets to earning long-term income through eCourses. Within these lessons, you'll learn ways to scale your business and sell higher-priced gigs without being overwhelmed. In addition, you'll learn to implement and drive relationship selling rather than force the scarcity mentality of selling.

If your day is fully booked and you don't have another billable hour to sell, this book is for you. If you are looking for ways to sustain your business, this book is for you. If you are looking for ways to scale your business, then yes, this book is for you. And if you hope to have more free time, increase your influence, and generate more revenue, you got it—this book is for you.

It's time to jump off the draining one-to-one client engagement cycle of running your business. Instead, build new income streams by using the proven systematic method outlined in this book to help you create your eLearning course or academy. This book will provide you with tips and techniques that you can use to start converting your intellectual capital into a revenue-generating machine immediately.

Our goal in writing this book is to help demystify the process of producing eLearning courses by giving you a straightforward, no-nonsense guide that will help you get started with confidence and have all the steps required to sell your eCourse. For clarity, this book is about scaling your business by adding a digital product to your service business. What it is not is a book about building a digital business.

This book uncovers the differences among eCourses, membership sites, and digital communities, and provides a brief note on webinars. It includes a proven business model for building a sustainable, scalable business by leveraging digital product offerings and teaches a systematic method for building an eLearning product that will help grow your business. We will expose ways to quickly implement technology products to help you automate your practice without adding frustration.

You Will Learn:

DISCOVERY: *Gain clarity on building a scalable business by integrating an eLearning course.*

- Be introduced to the eLearning industry.
- Build your scalable business model.
- Create a business plan.
- Identify and understand your target audience.

PLANNING: *Create a systematic outline for building a transformational eLearning course.*

- Choose the types of digital products you will incorporate, including communities and membership models.
- Create a course outline that is transformational.
- Select lesson components for consistency.
- Establish an eCourse name that resonates with your message.

DEVELOPMENT: *Develop the building blocks to help listeners easily gain knowledge and move through the course with ease.*

- Develop a course script that adds value to the listener.
- Create course enhancements to add to the experience.
- Select a technology platform and Learning Management System (LMS) that fits your business model.
- Receive tips on pricing an eCourse.

PRODUCTION: *Bring together everything that goes into the creativity, planning, and execution of the eCourse videos.*

- Learn voice-over tips and tricks.
- Find out filming hacks.
- Create a presentation that wows.
- Edit and produce the final product.

MARKETING: *Promote and sell eLearning products and other services.*

- Select a launch versus evergreen method.
- Become sales-ready by selling the course through follow-up.
- See how to drive traffic for upsells.
- Build automated campaigns.
- Format a video sales letter.

You will uncover all this information to create your digital product quickly and easily. Because you picked up this book, we know you're ready to scale your business and enjoy more free time than ever before—let's get started!

Part I

Move fast. A sense of urgency is the one thing you can develop that will separate you from everyone else. When you get a good idea, do it now.

BRIAN TRACY, INTERNATIONAL BUSINESS
COACH AND MOTIVATIONAL SPEAKER

CHAPTER 1
Revealing The Business Urgency

In a volatile world, "rigid" equals "brittle,"
and institutions that cannot figure out
how to work differently may not work at all.

PAUL LEBLANC, PRESIDENT OF SOUTHERN
NEW HAMPSHIRE UNIVERSITY

WOULDN'T YOU LOVE to tap into and profit from the multi-billion-dollar eLearning industry? It's possible.

Imagine waking up each day with more money in your bank account than when you went to sleep—only working with a select number of clients that pay you top dollar for your one-to-one interactions. Imagine closing more sales without selling by increasing your influence and leaving a legacy. If you capitalize on your experience, expertise, and aspirations, this can be your reality.

Your future in the digital space is exciting. Here's why:

First and foremost, let's reveal the most important things we've learned about scaling a business through digital products. Scaling a business can be as simple as thinking about business differently and acting differently through a newfound perspective and knowledge base. Everyone struggles with these ideas because throughout our entire consulting or coaching life, we focus on growing our business by providing superior customer service and superior customer service can only be given by being in person with a client. The truth is that being willing to shift our mindset and leverage technological advancement, plus using the proven solutions available, will allow coaches and consultants to work smarter in an ever-expanding borderless world.

We face shifts and interruptions more than we realize—it happens every day. Industry revolutions have shattered companies. Think online banking, access to movies, Amazon, travel, rideshare, and the list goes on and on. Industries that do not pivot and transform are crushed. Businesses need to rapidly shift into a kind of agile practice if they want to be sustainable and scalable. Gone are the days of long strategic planning and packets. It is time to change now—or it will be to the death of your business. There is a growing shift to abandon time for money. A successful company shares its message with a broader audience. Business owners need to monetize their intellectual capital to scale. A change in mindset with consideration for client-serving strategies needs to happen. A new business model will shift a business in this direction. How do we move into the new agile business model? By going digital.

Consider this. The digital eLearning industry will have grown to well over $325 billion by 2025.[1] More eLearning courses are being produced due to the high demand of listeners, not because of a business owner's choice. The consumer is driving the shift. Furthermore, it is unlikely the trend will end anytime soon.

---

[1] T. J. McCue, "e-Learning Climbing to $325 Billion by 2025 UF Canvas Absorb Schoology Moodle", July 31, 2018. Accessed May 29, 2022, https://www.forbes.com/sites/tjmccue/2018/07/31/e-learning-climbing-to-325-billion-by-2025-uf-canvas-absorb-schoology-moodle/.

According to Global Newsweek, "experts speculate the mobile eLearning market will rise to $80.1 billion by 2027."[2]

eLearning is unlike in-person learning, where spending money on booking a presentation room, providing food, and offering the course at a specific time and date is the norm. Additionally, everyone needs to travel, adding additional costs. eLearning courses, any digital products and automation allow people to learn anywhere and any time of the day. The exact time and money savings apply to you—you can be anywhere offering your digital products and services anytime, reducing the cost of doing business. Since the consumer demand for learning anywhere and anytime has exploded, the need to convert your content and digitize yourself is imperative—it is the only way to sustain, scale, and be relevant in this changing world.

Before we jump into the how-to sections, let's talk about some common barriers to moving forward.

The most significant barrier we found for people jumping into this growing field is fear of the unknown and its meaning to your current business model. For some, it is difficult to understand what it means to scale a business by adding digital products, what it means to generate passive income, and how to systematize a business. It is hard for some to accept that the time has come to pivot. Here is a list of common points of confusion that hold many people back from starting and, frankly, finishing their products.

Consider these barriers that you may face as you contemplate adding digital products to your offerings:

- fear of the unknown and feeling stuck

- believing there is only one way to build an eLearning course

[2] Report Link, "Global Mobile Learning Industry," August 18, 2020. Accessed May 29, 2022, www.globenewswire.com/news-release/2020/08/18/2080347/0/en/Global-Mobile-Learning-Industry.html.

- lack of technology expertise
- thinking it is too late to join the eLearning space
- information overload
- you do not know where to start
- confusion about building a digital product for business scalability versus building a digital business

Does any of this sound familiar to you? In this book, we will teach you the secrets to eliminating those barriers and break it down for you.

If you aren't convinced you need to go digital, let's talk about how you are currently doing business.

First, assess your day. Many coaches and consultants work all day with their clients and then come home (or stay at the office) to sit down to do all the paperwork and finish the follow-up required from the day's work. Do you ever get overwhelmed with the amount of work you have to do after 5:00 p.m.?

How about this—do you have a client that takes up a lot of your time but isn't paying you the money you deserve? We sometimes take on clients knowing that it's going to be a lot of work, but cash flow is tight, so we take them on. Or have you ever received a call from a friend, and they want you to give their friend a discount for services? Ugh.

What about having to manage all the rote work? Conducting a client intake? Teaching them your method? The intake is the same for every client, but it isn't inspiring or motivating when you engage with a new client. You want to do the exciting deep one-to-one work and get paid for your higher-priced packages. We've been there ourselves.

Are you tired of hearing, "I want to work with you, but I can't afford your program"? This one I hear a lot: "I hate sales calls." But what if you could say yes to them, without discounting, and still provide them with value, all the while creating the possibility of them buying from you later? This isn't only possible; it's doable. It's about managing the sales cycle differently.

We are here to help demystify the process and teach you how to scale your business easily and effortlessly by creating a new business model that incorporates eLearning courses and academies. We will show you a systematic step-by-step method for developing your eCourse, explain the ease of creation and production, and decode the technology. We will share ways to reduce your efforts—from concept to completion to launching your product—faster than you ever thought possible.

Take Action

What are the barriers that are holding you back from creating your digital product?

What actions do you need to take to overcome the barriers?

CHAPTER 2

The Confusion About Building
A Digital Business Model

*The people who are crazy enough to think they
can change the world are the ones who do.*
STEVE JOBS

L ET'S GET MOTIVATED. First, let's look at the 100x formula.
The 100x formula indicates that if you sell one hundred
courses at one hundred dollars each, you generate $10,000
in revenue. However, what if you price your course at $200?
Suddenly, you double your earnings to $20,000. Sounds won-
derful, right? That's not all there is, though. Several key factors
go into developing and marketing an eCourse to scale your
business and transform your clients.

The Business Flywheel Model

What we are talking about is adding digital products to
scale your business. How is this done? We create eLearning
courses, academies, or other digital products to generate revenue, generate leads, save time, and share our message with a

broader audience. It helps eliminate repetitive activities, such as sharing a framework or process, increasing knowledge or teaching something new, or automating employee training.

It is about digitizing yourself for value delivery and creating something for lead generation and revenue generation. It allows you to expand your reach, get further into a geographical location, or serve more clients. There is no limit to your growth.

A great example is Amazon's flywheel. Amazon first selected a small selection of products—books, to be exact. Customers purchased the items, and the customers' experience was positive.

Then, Amazon introduced more product selections, bringing more traffic to their site. Amazon found more sellers and created an even more fantastic selection of products. The continuous chain of events is known as the business flywheel. The flywheel process is how they created the Amazon conglomerate.

ADAPTED FROM AMAZON'S FLYWHEEL

The Myth Of One-to-One

What is the myth of one-to-one? The myth is that a single person can create a scalable business with one-to-one consulting or coaching. It says, provide value, provide a customer experience, and the client gets results, then the coach gets referrals. Voilà. This is how you envisioned your business would grow.

ONE-ON-ONE CONSULTING MYTH

ADAPTED FROM AMAZON'S FLYWHEEL

Myth busted—this isn't how it worked out. Here is how coaching and consulting practices work.

With one-to-one consulting, the more customers you serve, the worse the customer's experience will be. You're reducing the time you spend with your client. Therefore, you're reducing the level of service you provide for your client. You are not increasing the client experience. You are diminishing the client's experience, which leads to reduced client results, and with a lack of results, they will not refer you. Your flywheel will not propel you to success. Instead, it will crumble and fall apart. Your flywheel breaks!

FLYWHEEL BREAKDOWN

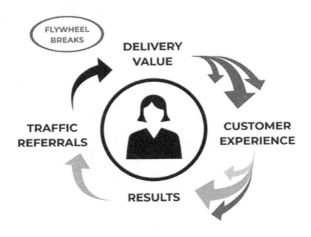

ADAPTED FROM AMAZON'S FLYWHEEL

As consultants, we all face the reality that we went into business to control our time, have freedom, and earn money. Yet, we are overworked, have no free time, and have capped out our earning potential. We are disappointed with more clients because more clients lead to less time and reduced freedom. Or we feel desperation because, on the other hand, the fewer clients we have, the fewer dollars earned. Either way, we get frustrated. That is why building your online course or a digital product is so critical to scaling your business.

The Benefits Of Digital Products

When John called us, he was running out of time in the day to manage all his incoming client inquiries. John is a career consultant helping people in their career transitions. His process was to work with individuals one-to-one in forty-five-minute sessions, usually for eight weeks. Before each client session, he would spend fifteen minutes preparing for the call; then he would get on the phone with the client, spending ten to fifteen minutes explaining the phone call's purpose; then he would spend about thirty minutes diving into the actual coaching process. After each session, John would spend about thirty additional minutes writing notes and sending an email to the client listing the follow-up actions. When it was all said and done, it took him two hours for each client, and he was only charging for one hour. When we talked to John, we asked him about his goals for creating a digital product. Our inquiry led us to ask him what part of his process is the same for each of the eight sessions. What was repetitive, and what could be automated? What is the content of each session, and could any of the sessions be eliminated?

After careful analysis, we helped John create a digital product. John's digital product included a series of videos teaching his client his "coaching process," videos facilitating the step-by-step actions for the client to complete, and downloadable documents to help the client stay on track. John automated his process by creating the digital product, helping the clients prepare for each session before getting on the phone, and reducing his repetitive actions.

His product also reduced his work per client per week by forty-five minutes. When his client begins the live one-to-one sessions with him, the client is well prepared. The client is ready to dive into the actual work. John reduced the total length of sessions, now meeting with the client for forty-five minutes versus sixty minutes. With this newfound free time, John can serve more clients. Don't worry; he still provides his clients with extraordinary value. Oh, and John continued to charge the same fee.

Then we met Sarah, a proud mom of two teenagers and caretaker for her parents. She is a successful coach to coaches. What was her problem? She wanted to generate more revenue, but she needed to figure out a way to have free time to manage her parents' trips to the doctors and drive her kids to and from sporting events. When we first met Sarah, she indicated she truly felt she could only provide value to her clients by meeting with them in person. She loves the one-to-one interaction with her clients and didn't want to lose that connection. However, she remained curious and open to various options for creating a digital product.

During the discovery phase, Sarah explained her mid-level priced package was a five-week program offering two days per week, for a total of ten hours. She spent one hour on Mondays teaching the principles of her framework and then verbally explaining the action steps to her clients. Then on Wednesdays, she would have the clients ask questions about their action steps and spend time answering their questions from the previous session.

So, what did Sarah create? For us, the challenge was to help her create a digital product that met all her needs—more revenue, more free time, and still have an in-person component. She digitized her framework lessons, provided her coaching clients an automated process, and offered downloadable action sheets so that the client could work through them while listening to the course. She kept her five-week workshop, but we helped her create a digital component and cut her time in half—five hours versus ten hours.

During Wednesday's sessions, she provided what she called live office hours. When her clients showed up for office hours, they understood the framework, had worked through the downloadable action sheets, and could fully engage with Sarah for specific solutions to their issues. Besides reducing her time and effort, the bonus was that she could convert clients faster into her VIP package.

What about the consultant's and coach's sales cycle? Would it be worth the time it takes to build your eCourse never to have to hear "no" again? You know the unfortunate objection we have all heard—I can't afford it—which feels like rejection. Adding an eCourse, like in the following example with the Johansson business partners, can help you seamlessly close more deals.

We have all experienced the sales process, which is both challenging and frustrating; this is how the Johanssons were feeling. First, we discovered they have three packages they offered—bronze, silver, and platinum—with a five- to six-figure price tag. Their goal during the sales cycle is to convert a potential client into one of the programs, knowing most people choose the silver category. They are on a mission to help entrepreneurs develop an abundance mindset, and they hate when someone is unable to transform by going through one of their programs. Their big question is, "How do we scale our business and help more clients transform?"

We spent time with the Johanssons, working on a new package they could offer digitally. We helped them structure it into modules, lessons, and components. Then breaking it down further, we helped organize the script into easily consumable chunks for the listeners. We collaboratively created a storyboard for the videos to match their branding. The Johanssons added the new digital option to their sales conversations with potential clients.

The Johanssons still begin by asking the potential new client the same few questions. As the conversation continues, the potential client will eventually ask, "How much does it cost?" The Johanssons explain their three packages and share the cost for each. If the potential client purchases any of the three packages the deal is done. Yay. However, suppose the potential client objects to the price of the bronze, silver, or platinum pricing. The Johanssons don't go to a default of discounting, negotiating, or begging, but they don't say no either. The Johanssons simply say, "We also offer an eCourse that will give you valuable information." They sell the eCourse at a lower price point than their other packages.

Just because a client bought a digital product doesn't mean it is the end of the sales cycle. We helped the Johanssons create multiple opportunities during the eCourse for the new client to purchase one of their larger packages.

The three clients that we shared with you were able to sell the listener into their more powerful and higher-priced packages upon completion of the course. All three clients provided a transformational experience during the eCourse. They offered easy access to the buy button for their other packages. After the eCourse experience, the listener knows, likes, and trusts them. And the listener wants more.

Our goal for our clients is to help them create the best scalable business model, a digital product that wows, and an eCourse that helps the listener transform. We also want the client to leverage their digital product to create opportunities for selling their higher-priced packages. In addition, we have helped our clients with the following:

- Offer extreme focus on content that works for their avatar and can be translated into a *wow* product. An avatar is a representation of the perfect client.

- Sort through large amounts of intellectual capital and reduce it to a sellable digital product.

- Explain the ease of creating a digital product without the hassle of learning something new.

- Decode technology platforms that can often be overwhelming.

- Research the best technology that suits the needs of the business model.

- Unlock ideas to produce the product, with no need to be an editing expert.

- Share ways for recording voice-overs and filming videos with or without a professional studio and expensive equipment.

- Expedite the learning curve and reduce the time from concept to completion during the launch of a digital product.

- Create Systems to scale the business by integrating digital products and automate.

In this book, we will share the tips and tricks in the above list so you can move into the digital arena with confidence. You have expertise that can benefit your clients, and you owe it to others to share your message with a broader audience.

Take Action

What are five digital product ideas you have thought about creating?

1.

2.

3.

4.

5.

Keep these ideas in mind as you continue to read, learn, and take action throughout the book.

Part II

The great aim of education is not knowledge but action.
HERBERT SPENCER, ENGLISH PHILOSOPHER,
BIOLOGIST, ANTHROPOLOGIST, AND SOCIOLOGIST

CHAPTER 3

Unraveling The Confusion About eLearning Courses, Membership Sites, And Online Communities

eLearning doesn't happen—it requires careful planning and implementation.
ANONYMOUS

A DIGITAL PRODUCT ALLOWS the transfer of knowledge to a client anytime, anywhere. It helps your client solve a problem and achieve transformational results. There are multiple types of digital products to choose from to produce and help your clients while expanding your reach.

This chapter will unravel the differences among eLearning courses, membership sites, digital communities, and briefly touch on webinars. We will explain when and why you should choose a single offering or leverage several types of products to scale your business. You will be taught everything you need to know to create a scalability model to fit your lifestyle. By the end of the book, you will have what you need to create an eye-popping, jaw-dropping eLearning course that sells and scales.

eLearning Courses

The term eLearning has become a broad, catch-all term used across all business sectors. For our purpose, an eLearning course is a transformational learning experience delivered electronically. Many elements can make up an eLearning program: live or prerecorded content, videos, quizzes, simulations, games, activities, and other interactive features. No matter what element you incorporate, it needs a wow factor.

Courses can be produced as a single topic or by combining multiple courses to make up an academy. They can be full-length multiple-hour lessons or shorter microlearning sessions. You can offer your eCourse via asynchronous or synchronous learning methods. It all depends on how your client consumes content.

There are multiple factors to consider when deciding to add an eLearning course to your products or services to maximize the return on investment. Do you want lead generation or revenue generation or to reduce time-intensive activity? It's important to know whether to use a lead generation or revenue generation strategy. Both are important but deciding which method fits your business model helps build a saleable course and focuses your marketing dollars on maximum returns.

Another important part of eLearning is to reduce time spent with your client in one-to-one sessions, which is a time-intensive interaction. It's not that we oppose one-to-one work, but rather that we are opposed to consultants and coaches tapping out their billable hours in the one-to-one format. If you choose to offer one-to-one consulting or coaching, higher-paying packages are reserved for those clients.

eLearning courses offer your potential clients a less expensive option to work with you. It gives a person the flexibility to transform anywhere, anytime. Adding a course to your offerings will help close sales more often because those who can't afford your higher ticket packages can still learn from you and transform—at a lower price point. It's a win-win.

The benefit to you is that the eCourse format is a highly sustainable and scalable business model, and it has the potential to scale globally.

When you choose to build your eLearning course, we won't sugarcoat it. There will be significant work upfront with little returns until after production, when your time and effort go down and rewards soar. If you follow the format in this book, you can easily create a course. We have had our clients go through our Course Class Systematic Method and launched in five weeks.

There is no standard rule for how long it takes to build an eCourse, but you should expect it to take approximately three hours for every hour of content. This formula includes ideation to creation to development through production. Don't let this discourage you. Just keep thinking, "I will have created something valuable for my clients and my business once finished, and I will have more free time and a product that can be repurposed and live on."

We think you can easily build an eLearning course or academy by drawing on your expertise, experience, and ambition.

Membership Sites

The difference between membership sites and digital communities often confuses people because the terms are often used interchangeably. We will clarify the differences between these two and explain each in more depth.

It is important to understand what a subscription membership site is and is not, so you can make a wise business decision on whether to add it to your scalable business model. Technically, a membership site is a non-brick-and-mortar business where a customer subscribes and gets access to content.

A membership model is an excellent online business to start and run, with an opportunity to build followers. A membership model is primarily a one-way conversation from the creator versus a digital community, which is a two-way conversation among the creator and members of the community. The membership site owner pushes the content out, and the member consumes the content.

Your membership site should include a variety of offerings that align with your membership model. A membership site's content can contain articles, blog-style articles, listicles, videos, podcasts, white papers, surveys, and more. You can offer webinars, live events, and free downloads within a membership site. Some types of content can also have forums, perks, or merchandise. You can use your membership site as an offshoot for your other digital products. This can include online courses, books, ebooks, and other content you have created. This could be your opportunity to upsell exclusive consulting and coaching packages, workshops, or retreats.

The emotional component of building a membership site can be advantageous for both you and the member. It needs to be so rich in information that your members are pleasantly anticipating the release of new content. The content needs to be alluring and make a personal connection with the member. Yes, you can make money if you consistently provide value to the member.

When should you build a membership site? Only start a membership site if you are ready to provide your customer with regular, consistent, and exclusive content. Content needs to be new and fresh daily, weekly, and monthly, and you must meet your avatar's needs. If you want to run an online business, are an authority in your field, want to build brand loyalty, or want to stay connected to a member base, then this model is for you. There are other specific benefits of a membership model. It builds a revenue stream, builds trust and loyalty, has low overhead costs, and requires little start-up funds. This model can increase your authority, build relationships, fulfill some gaps for members, and enhance value for your current clients.

Does a membership site sound like something you may want to add to your model? Keep it in mind when you begin to build your scalability model. Let's move on and talk about building a digital community.

Digital Communities

Communities are all around us. We're all part of many communities; they are family, friends, or a group of people with shared interests. Digital communities take on similar philosophies from an in-person community and translate them into a virtual format.

Most people are involved in a digital community, which includes belonging to a Facebook or LinkedIn group or another type of group that gathers virtually. You can offer various interactions, including selling your other digital products: eLearning, consulting, and coaching within a digital community.

We think the term "community" has become a buzzword in many situations, causing a lot of confusion because the concept of building a digital community can feel like a fad and somewhat abstract.

A community is a gathering of like-minded people with shared interests and purposes. Communities are passion- and purpose-driven. Digital communities have core values and engagement. The biggest difference between a membership subscription model and a digital community model is the presence of peer-to-peer learning in a digital community.

A digital community:

- builds engagement and learning
- empowers collective support
- shares a purpose and creates connections among members
- offers peer-to-peer learning
- stands out from the competition with an enhanced customer experience
- drives revenue growth for both the owner and the participant
- earns referrals and creates loyalty through customer advocates
- expands an organization
- invests in shared growth

The power of an online community can create continuous, meaningful interactions between and among members. These interactions will open the door to an incredible transformation for your business.

As you contemplate your options, we hope this helped shed light on the vast opportunity to go digital, whether you build a membership site or digital community, and how you can leverage your eLearning course as a standalone platform or otherwise.

Next, we will describe webinars—this is not our production specialty, but at times we use this business model for our business. We feel it important to equip you with this information as to why people use a webinar strategy to generate leads.

Webinars

A webinar is a one-way communication lecture-type offering in video format, which can be live or prerecorded. The audience can only interact via a chat, and often the chat content is also prerecorded. Typically, the presenter never sees the audience, and the audience rarely sees the presenter. A term you might also hear is Live-inar, which is just a live virtual meeting but is similar in format to webinars. Live-inars are offered in real time and allow two-way communication and seeing one another.

Great webinar hosts leverage technology platforms and share PowerPoint presentations, videos, web pages, and other multimedia content. The intent of a webinar is primarily business-related and used to share knowledge and ideas and can also be used to get leads and make a sale to one of your preferred packages.

Webinars are a way to share your expertise and product offerings with all the participants attending the event.

Webinars can be an effective way to attract potential clients, allowing you to convert them into customers. Today, many people run seventy-five to ninety-minute webinars as a lead generation strategy. At the end of the presentation, there is a time-pressured sales offer.

Typically, webinars require participants to register. For that reason, webinars are a great list-building tool. Free webinars can be an effective use of your time, given the number of new prospects and quality leads they will generate. To make this a profitable option, you need many people to register, even if they do not all show.

The one big problem today is that people have gotten frustrated with the webinar process. You listen to seventy-five minutes of content that has little to no value, and then the last fifteen minutes is the sales pitch. If you have ever participated in a webinar, you feel the pitch coming—often it feels uncomfortable—but you stay out of curiosity.

Usually, the sales pitch comes with a "buy now at this one-time price" offer. It puts the buyer in a scarcity mode where everyone feels they are missing out. A webinar strategy might be right for you. Many successful consultants and coaches use this process to generate millions of dollars in revenue. Consider if this fits into your lead generation strategy. For us, we don't use a high-pressure low-value method webinar strategy lead generation model. We provide value to the participants. We want them to walk away with an actionable task and we keep it between sixty to seventy-five minutes with an offer into one of our products. We do not create webinars for others, just for ourselves, as our expertise is in building scalable business models and the production of eCourses and academies, membership sites, system automation, and digital communities.

You are ready to move on and build your scalable business model, equipped with a working knowledge of eLearning courses, membership sites, and digital communities.

Take Action

Which concept is the most interesting to you?
And why?

eCourse as a single course?

> Why?

eCourse as an academy?

> Why?

Membership site?

> Why?

Digital community?

> Why?

Webinar?

> Why?

CHAPTER 4

The Scalability Business Model Exposed

What really matters to accelerate a sustainable future is being able to scale up production volume as quickly as possible.
ELON MUSK

SCALING YOUR BUSINESS doesn't just happen by accident. Time, effort, and planning need to go into building a business model that is both sustainable and scalable. Many business owners' mindsets are focused on getting enough clients to scale their businesses. Or they think that when they generate more revenue, they can add to their staff. Or they believe that if they work harder and put in more hours, they can grow their business. While this thinking can last for a bit, there comes a time when burnout and frustration take hold—and they make you want to slip on your running shoes and head for the proverbial hills. We want you to run only on vacation or on the beach while your eCourse generates money for you.

This chapter will expose how to build a business model that sustains your business and quickly scales it.

Typical Consultant And Coach Business Model

The typical consultant and coach business model has been around for fifty-plus years. Here is how the flow works.

Lead Generation. Client acquisition is usually a zero-revenue-generating activity. You spend many hours marketing, sending out newsletters, developing leads, and networking. The exploratory call is a judgment call—do I like you, and what can you offer me? If they seem interested in you and what you can promise them, you ask if you can send a proposal or wonder if you should bring up your pricing model to close the deal. The discovery call in this model only leads to the proposal process, not to a sale.

Proposal. You spend hours writing the perfect proposal. You're thinking, "They will love this proposal, it's beautiful, I am brilliant, and they will buy." However, the reality is that you have roughly a fifty/fifty chance of landing the client. Someone else might swoop in and offer a lower priced package. Possibly the potential client got a call from their friend who knows someone, and they go with that someone else. But you're waiting. As you wait, there's nothing. You email the prospect to follow up but still nothing—silence. Yep, you know the feeling. You still haven't received a dime from the potential client for all your efforts and the time you spent writing and working on the deal.

Value Delivery. You begin to deliver value for the wise half of the fifty/fifty group who accept your proposal. Extraordinary value. Your clients love you. You are getting referrals and excellent written testimonials—you are happy. You can see the blocks of time in your calendar for the one-to-one meetings. You are on a roll, and the money hits your bank account. *More Work, Less Time.* Yeah, this sounds great. But you start to realize that the more clients you acquire, the less time you have. Your days turn into nights; your days and nights turn into weekends. Your fun and freedom are gone—this is not a sustainable or scalable model.

Lower Quality Delivered. You pride yourself on your quality of work. You hate missing client follow-ups. Missing deadlines keeps you up at night. But you're starting to slip. There's too much work, too much to keep track of. What your clients love about you is your dependability and your dedication to their success. Yet, your clients notice the inconsistency. You're feeling the pressure. You get upset that a low-paying client takes up a significant amount of your time and you begin to resent that client. You start losing your passion, and you begin to dislike what you are doing.

Loss of Clients. The cycle you're trapped in leads to poor results for your business and your clients. Delivering unsatisfactory results can affect the client experience. As a result, clients don't renew; they might choose to cancel your services. You will lose any opportunity to upsell the client into your VIP package. A compilation of data gathered by Marketingblog.com stated, "The probability of selling to an existing customer is 60% to 70%, while selling to a new prospect is only 5% to 20%."[3] They further indicated, "Loyal customers spend 67% more than new ones." This loyalty is why we are so passionate about helping business owners make a shift in their practice.

---

[3] Marius Kiniulis, "11 Customer Acquisition vs. Customer Retention: What Data Says?", Markinblog.com, June 6, 2021, https://www.markinblog.com/customer-loyalty-retention- statistics/.

ONE-ON-ONE CONSULTING CLIENT EXPERIENCE

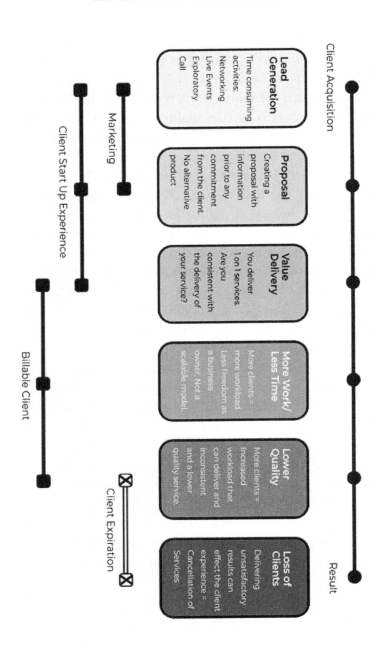

Client Acquisition

Result

Lead Generation
Time consuming activities:
Networking
Live Events
Exploratory Call

Proposal
Creating a proposal with information prior to any commitment from the client. No alternative product

Value Delivery
You deliver 1 on 1 services. Are you consistent with the delivery of your service?

More Work/ Less Time
More clients = more workload Less freedom as a business owner. Not a scalable model.

Lower Quality
More clients = Increased workload that can deliver and inconsistent and a lower quality service.

Loss of Clients
Delivering unsatisfactory results can effect the client experience = Cancellation of Services

Marketing

Client Start Up Experience

Billable Client

Client Expiration

Scalable Business Model

The scalable business model is about adding digital products to your offerings. In this model, you need to figure out how to leverage the digital product to achieve your desired outcome.

Before we break down this model, we want to address a few things first. We know there are two paths, a fork in the road. Business owners must choose when it comes to the online, virtual, eLearning stuff. They can choose to fight the change and stay the course, or pause, reflect, and use this book as a license to change.

Reimagine the nature of your work. Be open to the integration of a new idea. Accept that this is our life now: the digital age is here and will only accelerate. Here is why we think it is essential for you. According to an Accenture report, future-ready companies that doubled down on digital transformation and retooled have achieved about 7 percent more profitability—nearly twice the profitability of peers.[4]

Are you ready to consider a shift? Here is the model:

Lead Generation. You can expand your lead generation and increase your pipeline and geographic territory by offering a predetermined digital product. You can acquire potential clients by offering something for free, called a *freemium*. A freemium can be a downloadable document or video. This strategy is vital because it's all about email collection. You don't have to use a direct exchange of time for money because it is all

---

[4] "'Future-Ready Organizations Leveraging Digital to Operate Faster and Smarter Could Help Unlock $5 Trillion in Economic Growth," Accenture.com, January 27, 2021, https://newsroom.accenture.com/news/future-ready-organizations-leveraging-digital-to-operate-faster-and-smarter-could-help-unlock-5-trillion-in-economic-growth-says-accenture-study.htm?_ga=2.134776497.1387878364.1630029255-1938270173.1630029255.

automated, but it only works if you have created something of value.

Exploratory Call. You exchange your proposal writing time with a live call getting you closer to the sale. Exploratory calls are short, approximately fifteen to thirty minutes. The exploratory call is with a target-rich, vetted, interested person. During the call, you have an opportunity to sell a digital program or your higher-priced product. It is not about upselling; at this point, you are simply offering them options, whereas before, you offered them a proposal.

You can give your potential client options by providing a digital course, or maybe a book. The digital courses are accessible offerings that you can use to upsell your premium packages in the future. Another offer could be a virtual group or workshop with or without office hours. How about offering a community of like-minded people or a monthly membership subscription package?

Giving your clients digital options accelerates the sales cycle. Your client no longer must immediately choose whether to work with you at your high-priced package. They now have some options when they purchase a digital product. They get to know you. Then, they like you, and then they enjoy you even more. They grow to trust you and rely on you even more. By now, some of your clients will be in transition and ready to buy your premium package.

Giving your clients options is beneficial because they can choose how they want to work with you now and in the future. This model offers additional ways to interact with you. We give options because we believe in the customer's lifetime value.

Value Delivery. Digital products provide a consistent

product delivered at your client's convenience and on their schedule, not your schedule. It also helps the sales cycle by:

- generating more sales by offering a lower-cost product

- offering a more accessible entry point for potential clients to see if they like you

- overcoming the objection "I can't afford you"

- meeting the needs of the client's learning style and choice of level of engagement

- building a relationship-selling model

- creating a lifetime customer value proposition, as they might return and purchase your VIP package

More Clients And More Freedom. You went into business to generate revenue and have free time to do the things you love. You have reduced the sales cycle and time spent working one-to-one, and now you can sell your higher-priced packages.

High Quality. A digital product delivers a high-quality, consistent product and customer satisfaction.

Client Referrals. Consistency in the delivery provides an opportunity to upsell your VIP packages. You have courses, you have sales, you have results, and you have ambassadors who are referring others to your eCourse. All are leading to more sales, more results, more ambassadors, and it doesn't matter how many courses you sell. It doesn't matter how many participants purchase your eCourse; you keep delivering value.

ONLINE DIGITAL PRODUCT CLIENT EXPERIENCE

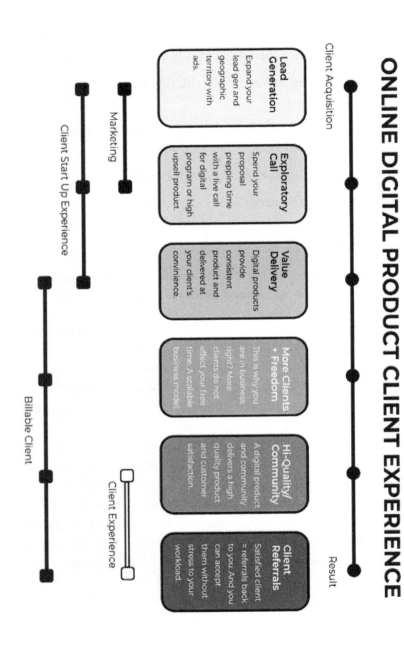

Client Acquisition

Result

Lead Generation

Expand your lead gen and geographic territory with ads.

Exploratory Call

Spend your proposal prepping time with a live call for digital program or high upsell product.

Value Delivery

Digital products provide consistent product and delivered at your client's convinience.

More Clients + Freedom

This is why you are in business right? More clients do not effect your free time. A scalable business model.

Hi-Quality/ Community

A digital product and community delivers a high quality product and customer satisfaction.

Client Referrals

Satisfied client = referrals back to you. And you can accept them without stress to your workload.

Marketing

Client Start Up Experience

Billable Client

Client Experience

Think back to the flywheel. Remember where the flywheel broke down? It was when you had more clients than time in the day, and you could no longer maintain your high level of service. By developing your scalability model, your flywheel will not break down. Your flywheel will propel your business to success.

The following four chapters will teach you how to build and produce your eLearning course.

Take Action

Draw your digital business model.

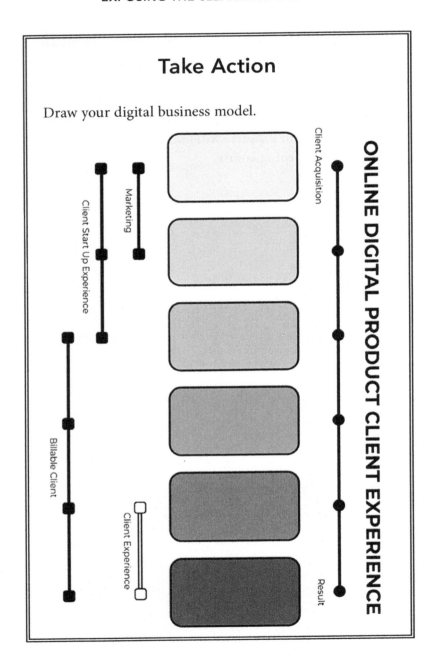

CHAPTER 5

Discovery: Gaining Clarity

I never dreamed about success, I worked for it.
ESTÉE LAUDER

NOW THAT YOU have learned about the consulting and coaching flywheel and started to develop your scalability model, you need to build a clear business plan. The plan will be your guide; it will help you stay on track as you create, produce, and market your eCourse in the shortest amount of time possible. This chapter will discuss the key points that go into writing your business plan. Before we start, it is essential to describe the four elements that make a successful eCourse.

Four Elements

What are the four elements required for a successful digital product? You must have a good instructor, great content, outstanding visuals, and fantastic audio. These components are equally important for the success of your course, which is only as good as the weakest of these four elements.

Instructor. Being an instructor for a digital product is not the same as standing in front of a room and presenting. Good instructors, facilitators, and speakers don't always make good online instructors. However, it is easy to learn and make the transition. Before you record audio or video, it's important to self-evaluate. Ask yourself, am I comfortable being on camera? Do you even want to be in front of the camera or behind the lens? Can you memorize your script, or do you want to read your notes while you present? Maybe you have all the content and expertise, but you choose to outsource the voice-over. Who are you as an instructor, and what is your preference?

Content. You may ask yourself, "Do I have enough expertise to create an eCourse?" Heck yeah, you do. Just think about how many days you have been here on this earth, how many hours, how many minutes you've spent honing your craft. Reflect on how much knowledge, experience, and research you have done over your lifetime. Yes, you are adept enough to create your online course. With all your knowledge, experience, research, and expertise, and using the framework in this book, you can easily break your product down into modules, lessons, and components. By following the framework outlined in this book, confusion in course creation is reduced so that the participant can effortlessly follow your lessons and understand your transformational message.

Visuals. The power of a visual is irrefutable. Creating visuals that resonate and connect with your avatar while presenting entertaining media can lead to the desired results. As a course creator, underestimating the importance of visuals that align with your avatar's liking can lead to a terrible outcome.

Audio. The most successful eLearning courses are all-encompassing and allow learners to become fully immersed in the learning process by utilizing a variety of multimedia elements. Excellent audio enables the learner to become fully engaged in the process. You'll want to record clear audio with minimal white noise. The recording should be well-paced, articulate, and express good diction. The best audio does not distract the listener from learning.

If you have terrific content but lousy video and audio or poor visual presentations, your course isn't that good. The participant will struggle while viewing or listening to your lessons. If your content is great, audio and presentation are stellar, but you as an instructor do not present well, trust can be broken. You may not engage your participants with your teaching style, or your participants may not continue with the course. When one of the elements is missing, you have failed to deliver on the intended outcome or transformation you intended for the participant. Without all four elements, your course may not lead to the success you desire; this is how our systematic method prepares you for creating your digital product and how to include all four elements.

Business Plan

It is time to create your eCourse business plan outline. You will complete a draft, and as you gain clarity throughout the book, you can further develop your plan.

Overview

First, you must identify your overarching goal for creating an online course. Is it for lead generation or for you to become a known expert or an influencer? Do you want to automate your processes? Maybe it's because you want to make an impact, or is the goal of your course revenue generation? Do you want to license your work to others? Create a certification program? It could be you want to share your experiences and leave a legacy.

Whatever it is for you, lead generation, revenue generation, or process automation, just know which one will work for you.

Here are three types of digital products you can create. You can choose them for lead generation or revenue generation. Maybe you want to do it for process automation. Before you read further, go back to your scalability model to make sure you're adding the correct type of digital product.

Lead Generation

For lead generation, a small digital product is developed that provides a lot of value to your potential customer. By offering a micro-digital product, your email list can grow, traffic is driven to your website, your brand identity is improved, and you have a product for all your social media platforms with an upsell offer to your other products and services. This will help you attract and transform online users into prospects for your business.

You can offer a freemium, a free ebook, or a ninety-nine-cent downloadable ebook. You can do a downloadable digital document or maybe a video, such as a video sales letter or an informational video. Perhaps you want to do a prerecorded webinar or lead qualifier. You can create a micro-eLearning course or offer one module for free.

Revenue Generation

Next is revenue generation, where the goal of your digital product is to make it a profitable piece of your business and build in opportunities for people to purchase your core business services. A bonus is you generate revenue from the sale of your digital products.

An eLearning business where you only sell eCourses is uniquely different than a business where you use digital products to grow your business. This is an important distinction, but the development principles of the products are the same.

If your business model is to simply sell courses, you need multiple courses to sell to generate substantial income and you need to spend a lot of money on marketing—this is your entire business. This book is about the latter, creating a scalable business model. Having people buy your eCourse and then upsell into your VIP packages. Or you are licensing your framework or course as we will discuss in Chapter 10.

When choosing a digital product to grow your business, you must be clear about your purpose and your business model. The idea is for you to sell the course for a great price point and then lead them to an upsell into your VIP package. In other words, you digitize your professional services or intellectual capital in some form adding a revenue stream with the goal of upselling your VIP packages. When attracting a new client to purchase your larger packages, selling a course for a nominal fee generates revenue directly from the sale. It also gives potential clients options if they aren't ready to buy your more expensive services. Importantly, if people get to know, like, and trust you as they go through your course, then they will more likely purchase your higher-ticket packages.

The advantage is that your buyer can work with you at different price points that are comfortable for them and anytime and anywhere convenient for them.

Systems Automation

There are two areas to look at a business for how to scale: either save time or generate more revenue. Saving time allows for more energy to focus on other parts of your business and more personal time. More revenue leads more opportunities for business growth and building a lifestyle for the business owner. Systems automation is as important as revenue generation.

Process automation of digital products helps standardize some processes in your business. For example, is your client intake process the same for all your clients? What if you automated the process? Then the first face-to-face meeting allows you to jump into the depth of the work. Or if you are onboarding an employee, you could create a course that explains how to accomplish the task associated with the role. What can you simplify in your client onboarding process or your product and service training for either an internal market or external market? Maybe you can automate the necessary marketing tasks, repetitive activities, or company-wide communication. By digitizing some of these repetitive actions, your business saves time.

Many people don't think they can digitize their services. But it is possible and worth it. Let's take an example of an attorney, whose first session was a general meeting about who the attorney is, how they will work with their client, the attorney's client process, and an explanation of paperwork. What's key about digitization is that the business owner is not doing one-to-one, face-to-face consultations.

The attorney's first meeting is usually about a thirty-minute consult. So what? It's only thirty minutes. True, but remember it is thirty minutes that the attorney can be billing another client. The attorney digitized the consult and now delivers the message on a TV in the conference room, where there is water, snacks, pens, and paper. The person listening can begin to get their thoughts down on paper and write down their questions for the attorney. While the client watches the video, the attorney works on another case file and has billable hours on that case. Their free non-revenue-generating activity of thirty minutes with the client generates revenue. The consult went from a non-revenue-generating activity to a revenue-generating activity, right? How sweet is that?

This concept is just one way to scale your business. This same attorney went further and offered a do-it-yourself eCourse option. It's a self-service option for someone who cannot afford a full attorney rate, eliminating the "no" in the sales cycle.

Customer onboarding is another non-revenue-generating activity. Everyone onboards customers in some way. Ask yourself, how could you automate the process of customer onboarding? Coaches and consultants, your first meeting with a client usually is identical every time—you have a set of inquiry questions. You begin by gathering general information to help you best serve the business owner. The first session is, on average, sixty minutes and is a great way to start digitizing and automating.

Creating a video is an excellent way to digitize yourself, as it gets the client engaged with you. You can create downloadable forms for them to work on before the first session. When digitizing yourself, you should share why the video and documents are essential to review and explain the importance of offering a digital format. For example, you can say, "Thank you for watching the video and filling in the forms. This prep work will better prepare me to serve you well at our first face-to-face meeting." Believe it or not, it does your client no good for you to ask them questions on the first call just to gather information. It's boring, and they pay you to present them with ideas and feedback. They want you to provide value from the start.

It's also important to know that you're giving the client all the information they need to work with you when you digitize yourself. Explain how you work and when and where they can find time to work with you. Share your entire process of the engagement or your framework. Talk about expectations for working together. We find that many times as business owners, we get the deal, and we forget to educate the customers on what experience they're going to receive. Why not help them to be successful with you? Digitize.

Digitizing gives all your clients the same consistent customer experience. For example, what's a client call like on Monday morning? It's great. We are ready to go because we've got all this energy. We know we are hitting the mark and firing on all cylinders.

It's the end of the week. Things have been good, but we've had some bumps in the road. Face it; we are all kind of tired. Maybe we aren't as "put together" as we were on Monday morning. We leave things out and maybe can't articulate as well. What about onboarding a client at four o'clock on a Friday afternoon? It's not fair to the Friday client—give every client an equal opportunity to see you at your best.

Digitize your business to present the best of you each time.

Content

Stating the obvious, you have a lot of content in your head you can choose to share. The hard part is deciding what content you want to convert into your digital product. To get started, here are important questions you should ask yourself:

- What content do you already have available?

- Can you digitize a part of your one-to-one service?

- Do you already have a workshop you can digitize?

- Can you convert a book into a digital product?

- Do you have a speech?

- What problem is your course solving?

- Do people spend money on the topic?

- What are you an expert at doing or teaching?

- What do others think you are talented at doing?

Narrowing it down can be difficult. But there is always another course in you. Keep in mind the second, third, and fourth digital product is easier to create than the first. That means you don't have to, nor should you, include everything in the first go around.

Outcome

Knowing who you want to write the course for makes it easier to build your product with precision and focus. Take a few moments to write down several sentences for each of these essential overarching questions:

- Who is your course for?

- Who is your audience?

- What is the desired outcome of your course?

- After a person takes your course, what new skills will they have?

As you develop your course, often refer to the "who and what" you have indicated. The more you stay on target, the quicker you can write your script and produce your product.

Product(s)

What do you think you would like to create? What type of specific product makes the best sense to accomplish your goals? Briefly note your answers to each of these questions. Is it:

- a training course, academy, or freemium?
- a video sales letter?
- one course or multiple courses?
- an eLearning academy?
- a mini- or microcourse?
- a membership site, or do you want to build a community?
- a certification program or licensing your framework?

Don't get into the paralysis-by-analysis mode as you work through these questions. Identify what you are thinking, and as you continue to learn, you can make a well-informed decision that's right for you.

Production

When it comes to production, don't ruminate on *how*. We don't want the fear of producing a product to stop you from adding a digital product to your business model. We will share tips and tricks to make it painless. And if you decide to hire someone to produce your course, we provide you with enough information to ask the right questions to hire the right production company. As an organization, we pride ourselves on spending a lot of time with our clients untangling the process for production to help put their minds at ease. When our clients reach out and talk to us for the first time, this is the area that causes the most confusion and angst.

For example, think about if you want to create a slide deck with a voice-over. Do you want it to be all video, or will it be mixed media? Write down your answers and what you are leaning toward doing.

Pricing Model

The question is, "What should you charge for your product?" And it is crucial to ask.

Here's what to consider with your pricing model. What length will your course be? What was your strategy for creating your course? Was it for lead generation, revenue generation, or process automation? Work backward. What is the value of the outcome, and what price would they pay for the outcome you promise? What is your competitor charging? What are alternatives to meet the needs of your avatar? Where would they go, and what would they pay to get the same information?

Are you a known expert on the topic? Provide options and different price points. For example, a complete marketing course offered for $250 or three smaller courses on a specific marketing topic for $100 each. Leverage scarcity and make your reduced pricing count. If you choose to discount your course, reduce your offering. Don't get hung up on your pricing; you can test it because no one will compare what others have paid when the course is offered on the internet.

Here's how to increase the value of your online course:

- Teach something very specific.

- Create a private group.

- Offer downloadable resources.

- Let them know if you are open to a payment plan.

Are the students going to have access to you? Can you add or upsell your one-to-one coaching, and host monthly live calls, webinars, or memberships? Form partnerships to give your students extra resources. Offer course completion certificates.

Go back and visit the goal of your course. Was it designed for lead generation, or were you going to sell a high-ticket product?

Depending on your goal, if it were lead generation for free or a low entry price, you would have more sales, but if it were a high-ticket item, you would probably have fewer product sales. A lower price or higher price isn't right or wrong. It's important to understand the sales volume compared to the price point. We suggest you go back to your scalability model and see where your price point fits into your model.

Avatar

Identifying your avatar is necessary. Often business owners skip the process of detailing their client avatar. Some owners believe their products and services are so good that they will reach the masses. Not true. Or the business owner has what is called FOMO: Fear of Missing Out on finding clients, and dollars are left on the table if they exclude anyone from their offer. It's quite the opposite—go broad, go broke. If people take the time to write a list of attributes about their avatar's preferences, often it is superficial at best. For your eCourse, identifying your avatar must be taken seriously. The success of your eCourse depends on how well you know and understand the likes and dislikes of your avatar.

Here are a few questions you should answer and research your ideal avatar if necessary. List your answers to the following:

- Who is the target audience you want to sell your course to?

- What visuals does your avatar enjoy watching?

- How does your avatar like to receive information?

- Is your avatar the creative, artistic type?

- Does your avatar prefer bright colors or natural colors?

- Are they drawn to a structured industrial look?

- Do they like an informal look with a lot of animation?

- What are your avatar's likes and dislikes?

- What do they read for business and pleasure?

- Are they playful, artsy, or formal?

- What are their values, interests, and lifestyle?

- What music do they listen to?

- Who is your avatar?

Understanding your avatar, from the foods they like, where they go, and who they follow, will become important when you enter production.

Now that you have studied the four elements of a great course, built your business plan, and identified your avatar, let's move on to the planning phase.

Take Action

Identify the purpose of your digital product:

- lead generation
- revenue generation
- process automation

Answer the following questions:

- Who is your course intended to serve?

- Who is your audience?

- What is the desired outcome of your course?

- After a person takes your course, what new skills will they have?

- Who is your ideal client?

CHAPTER 6

Planning: Creating A Systematic Outline

I've learned that people will forget what you said, people will forget what you did, but people will never forget how you made them feel.

ATTRIBUTED TO MAYA ANGELOU

GET READY; THIS chapter is all about designing your course. We will cover how to prepare your content and show you how to organize your course into modules, lessons, and components. We will give you tips on selecting and outlining your course. Then, we will share how to develop a kick-ass course name.

Designing Your Course

Courses are the overarching digital online product, where modules are your high-level topics, and lessons are your subtopics for each module. When designing your course, it is essential to stay consistent with your terminology. To teach you how to design your course, we will use the terms "course," "module," and "lesson." When designing your course, you may choose to use these terms or be more creative. For "course," you may want to use "academy" or "track." For "modules," you can use "level" or "path," and "lesson" could be "session" or "class." Whatever terms you use, make them consistent throughout your course. When designing the flow of your course, it is important to select the type of components you want to use. Components are in the main body of your course outline.

There is no firm rule on how long an online course should be, but here are some averages: the average course is about four to six modules. The modules contain four to six lessons each, and the lesson duration could be a few minutes or up to twenty minutes, never longer. A caution here: some Learning Management Systems restrict the length of your videos per lesson. Any longer than twenty minutes, you may lose your participants' attention, or they could start multitasking during a long lesson.

How long is it going to take? For one hour of course content, it will equal about eight to ten hours of designing and writing, plus time for recording and producing your work. We won't sugarcoat the truth: there is high effort and low return when developing the entire course. However, the completed course will show low effort with high return. Stay motivated and trust the framework we created.

Selecting Your Course

Start by knowing what you love to teach. Think back and identify what others have said they want to learn from you. Pick a niche. Identify your avatar. Know if your goal is to help your avatar overcome a challenge, build a skill, or change a habit.

Now that you are clear on your niche, let's find out what the competition is doing. Check out other online courses and take a course. You might find other courses like yours, which is good because that usually means there is a high demand for your topic. Understanding what the competition is doing helps create your unique message. You will use your stories, delivery style, and personality to craft something meaningful for your avatar. Gaining clarity on your competitors only helps you develop, name, and price your course.

Preparing Your Content

Here are a few things to keep in mind when designing your content. Your number one goal in creating your online course is to take the participant to the desired outcome quickly and efficiently. People will buy your course because of the promised transformation. You are the expert and have a lot of knowledge and experience, and have researched your topic, but don't give the participant information overload. Please don't take the last twenty years of your life and provide them with everything you know at once. Stick to your content plan when developing your course. Be focused and keep the end in mind.

The path model represents the steps participants will take in your online course. The first step would be to understand the current situation of your avatar. After the final lesson, they should achieve their desired results or outcome. After they take your course, ask yourself what your avatar can do now that they couldn't do before they took your course. You should write this down as a reminder: "My job as a course creator is to take them from the current situation as quickly and efficiently as possible to the desired result."

Organizing Your Content

When organizing your content outline into the main topics or modules, begin at the end. Your last module should be the content closest to the desired result. For example, let's say you're creating a course on "How to Lose Twenty Pounds in Sixty Days." The current situation is that someone is probably overweight, and their desired result is to weigh less or lose twenty pounds. The last module could be something like "How to Lose the Last Difficult Five Pounds" or "Now You Have Lost the Weight, How Do You Maintain It?"

Once you have the main topic of your final module, you will create your other module topics. Then, add your lesson subtopics under each module. With your main module topics and lesson subtopics written down, you will break down a lesson into components. Components are the real guts of your online course.

There are various components you can use to deliver your lesson content. But before we share the specific elements, it is essential to understand why it is so important to use the components model for course design. Components allow you to deliver your information logically, sequentially, and consistently. You're setting clear objectives. You prepare the learner with the necessary materials for the course, giving them clear, direct instructions, providing background knowledge of the content, and demonstrating how it works. Your course should have a consistent flow, as the learner needs to understand how to learn what you are teaching.

Here are some components you can use:

- Welcome them to the lesson or session.

- Introduce yourself as the instructor.

- Share the course outline.

- Deliver your general content.

- State a definition.

Here are some additional lesson components to engage your audience:

- Give an example.

- Explain the history of your content.

- Use a visual diagram to explain your content.

- Show a photo while telling a story.

- How about a list?

What about using a motivational quote, a cartoon, or referencing an article? Insert something funny to grab their attention. You can review the content of what you just covered in the previous lesson, tell them what is coming next, suggest what they can expect to look forward to, and explain how to close and sign off at the end of the lessons and modules. Select the components to standardize your lessons.

Let's go back to the weight loss example. Maybe the main topic in Module 2 is exercise, so the subtopic for Lesson 1 could be exercising at the gym. The subtopic for Lesson 2 could be exercising at home.

The welcome component might sound like this: "Welcome to the next lesson on how to exercise efficiently at home. I'm your fitness instructor. In this lesson, we will cover how to exercise at home with equipment and without." Here you would transition into delivering some general content. You might choose to deliver some video examples of how to do the exercises. Then, you could provide them with a list of daily exercise routines.

As you move to the close, you might want to say: "Make sure you stay consistent in your exercise. Continue on your weight loss journey." As you can see, components let the learner know where you are taking them and helps them follow along. Don't be cryptic in your messaging.

Although we like to use components for consistency, don't fall into the component trap. Sometimes you must change it up a little. Be entertaining. Don't leave any questions unanswered. Remember, you don't have a live audience. They can't ask you questions, so be sure you're clear and consistent.

Outlining Your Course

When outlining your course, make sure you know the definitions for modules, lessons, and components, as we will expand a bit. We know our course creator clients did their research before coming to us and explored other course developers. We know other experts have different ideas and thought processes. But for us, we're clear on what works best for authors, speakers, coaches, and consultants.

First and foremost, what comes first, the outline or the ideas? We believe the outline, always the outline. Creating an online course isn't a brain-dump session with yourself. It's not about buying a lot of Post-it notes and writing everything you know about the subject, and then having a hundred nonsensical Post-it notes on your wall. If you have something that doesn't fit your lesson, jot it down and put it in a file because guess what? There's another course in you. There's a second course, a third course, maybe more. Don't deliver all your brilliance in your first course. We have found the Post-it note thing gets course creators overwhelmed. We are here to take the overwhelmingness out of creating an eLearning course.

Sometimes course creators let their egos get in the way. They have so much information and attach it to an emotion. They do the brain dump and throw every morsel of knowledge up on the wall. We say these people have "hopium"—I hope it works out. I hope everything I'm delivering to the client they will understand; I hope someone will buy my course. I hope. I hope. I hope. Knowing what you know now, you will plan your course correctly, so you don't need hopium. You know what results the participants need, and it's your responsibility to give them to them.

Naming Your Course

You've outlined your course, and you have a general idea of the content. It's time to develop your kick-ass name. Choosing a title is one area in course creation that can challenge the creator. Here are some tips: be specific and narrow. Remember the outcome for the participant. Make it short, catchy, and to the point. Again, it should be outcome driven. What can they do now that they couldn't do before taking your course? Naming the course "How to Lose Twenty Pounds in Sixty Days" is concise. Many people want to be overly creative with developing their course name—don't. Clarity will always win over cleverness.

Here's what's important. When buyers read the title, they need to know what's in it for them. They should know what it's about and what the outcome is. The title should be short and to the point. Two sentences max; the title is two to three words, and the subtitle is seven to ten words. Shorter is better. The subtitle is for clarity and context of your title, including the standouts, transformation, results, and desired future state. Adding a timeframe for the desired outcome is usually best.

Make it benefit-driven. The participants should understand what's in it for them and focus on the value that you provide them. Think of your avatar but have fun with it. Elicit emotions through words such as jump-start, quick start, ultimate, tricks, new, amazing, and awesome. What buzzwords would connect with your avatar?

Some of you may have a workshop or keynote speech you're transforming into an online course. Maybe you already have a book. These can be converted easily into an eLearning course, as you already have content. But when it comes to naming your course, the rule of thumb is never to name your course the same thing as your workshop, keynote, or book title— never, ever. You will confuse the buyer.

Here's a quotable quote, "Confused buyers never buy." If you have a book titled *How to Sell to Anyone* that you're selling for twenty dollars, and you have a course with the same title for $147, suddenly the buyer wonders, "Which one should I get? I don't know which one is better for me." You'd be lucky if they even spent twenty dollars to purchase your book at that point. You can have the same content; just name it something different.

What's nice about having a book is that you have material for multiple courses. We found that people can take their book, use chapters of the book to make multiple courses, give each course a different title, and bundle three courses together and offer them all for sale.

Before you create a name, be clear on who it is for by using this formula:

My course (working title) helps (group/avatar) learn how to (what you are specifically going to teach) so they can (results they will get, what they will be, do, or have after taking your course).

Then use one of these naming templates:

- How to get (desired outcome) without (usual problem).
- (Number of) simple steps to (desired outcome) without (usual problem).

Here are a few examples:

- How To Make Money While You Sleep In Thirty Days Or Less.
- How To Write Your Smashing Article In Forty-Eight Hours.
- How To Hire A Virtual Assistant In The Next Seven Days.

Create about five sample titles, then do a survey and ask people to read each title and give you feedback on what they think the course is about. Adjust and test again. Once you feel you have the correct title, go for it. Remember, cleverness over clarity never works.

The next chapter is on development. We will break down the scripting process and talk about a production schedule and downloads. We will also give you suggestions on how to price your course.

Take Action

Start developing your outline, using the template below:

Module 1 Title: _____

Lesson 1 Title: _____

Lesson 2 Title: _____

Lesson 3 Title: _____

Module 2 Title: _____

Lesson 1 Title: _____

Lesson 2 Title: _____

Lesson 3 Title: _____

Module 3 Title: _____

Lesson 1 Title: _____

Lesson 2 Title: _____

Lesson 3 Title: _____

CHAPTER 7

Development: Building Blocks For Success

A word after a word after a word is power.
MARGARET ATWOOD

IN THE PREVIOUS chapter, we went over planning. We showed you how to break down and outline your course into modules, lessons, and components. This planning phase is a critical step before digging into the development phase of your course. A clear course breakdown and outline such as the one you created in Chapter 6 will help you accelerate the action to take in this chapter on development.

In this chapter, you will develop your course script, create enhancements, and use downloadable documents as a value add. We will also discuss building your course production schedule.

As you develop your course, we know this part of the process is where our course creators often get overwhelmed. Because of this overwhelmingness, we created a step-by-step process allowing you to script your course easily and quickly—development is a heavy lift.

Writing A Script

When developing your course script and methods to provide the client experience, there are critical rules to follow.

Timing. Lessons should be less than twenty minutes, but they can be as short as a few minutes. You want to break up the content into easily manageable chunks. Following these rules is essential for three reasons:

1. The learner learns better in small chunks.

2. Learning Management Systems allow video uploads of less than twenty minutes.

3. It will easily enable the listener to access the lessons.

Language. There are so many ways to express ourselves when we are trying to communicate our message, but when you write your script, you should be hypersensitive to the language you use. Don't use words that people won't understand or have difficulty relating to. If you're using a term specific to your industry, define it. In addition to explaining terms, it is best not to use lingo, fancy words, or abbreviations as the listeners will disengage—if in doubt, write it out.

Clarity. We all have certain words that, for some reason, under pressure, we can't say with clarity. If you have one of those words that challenge you, we suggest not using it and finding a different one. Next, be careful how certain words are pronounced and how the words will be heard through audio. Be clear when talking about "it," "they," or any reference to a subject. Don't assume the listener will understand your reference. Don't make the listener have to decode your message.

Questions. This one can prove to be complicated. As you are writing your script, don't leave any questions unanswered. Remember, your listeners can't raise their hands to ask you questions. So, be sure to answer anything that might leave your listener hanging and saying to themselves, "Hmm, I wonder what that means?"

Time Stamping. When writing your script, you should remove any references to a specific date, time, or season. You wouldn't want to say it's raining today, repeat something newsworthy, or use a current event unless your course is a solution to the recent event. By not time stamping, you are preserving the course and its longevity. No matter who registers, or when they join or listen, the material isn't outdated.

Infotainment. Suppose you have chosen to develop a slide presentation with a voice-over (converted into a video) for your course. In that case, you need to ensure that your audience is "infotained" and "edutained." You're probably wondering what the heck we mean by "infotained" and "edutained." Infotainment combines information and entertainment, and edutainment combines education and entertainment. That's what you want to do as you build your course script. You want to provide extraordinary value through the information you share while keeping the listener listening by presenting the information and education in an entertaining way. You need to understand the basics of writing a great script. When you write your script and develop a slide presentation, you want to ensure your participants are not bored.

Visuals. Don't hang out on the same slide for more than a minute—remember you will convert the presentation into a video, and a minute is a very, very long time to the viewer. If you think your content will cover a few bullet points and you will talk for about ninety seconds to two minutes, break up the slide. You can break it up into four different slides. One slide will have the header or your topic, and then you want to create another slide with point one, another side with point two, and so on. Technically, you will have four different slides for a ninety-second script, but it will be much smoother when you're recording and the viewer is watching it. You don't want to pack too much information on one slide; spread it over multiple slides. In your script, the standard rule is to use short segments because the time spent on a slide should not exceed one minute.

Have you ever gone to a presentation where you tried to read the material without success? Was the writing tiny because they put too much on the slide or had too many graphics? It is difficult and frustrating to follow along. Make your slides clean and simple for the listener to effortlessly follow along when they're watching the video.

What does this mean? If you write your script to be infotainment, you might have three animated slides for every sixty seconds of a lesson; therefore, in a five-minute lesson you could have fifteen to twenty slides. Taking it one step further, for a one-hour course, if you did only one slide per minute, you would have sixty slides—most likely even more. Please, don't feel overwhelmed. The overwhelmingness is why we prefaced this phase as a heavy lift. Rest assured we will share some tips and tricks in the production chapter to make it easier than it sounds. For now, concentrate on writing a fantastic script for each lesson.

Enhancements

Course enhancements are the glitter and sparkle, thus giving your course the wow factor. Enhancements shouldn't add work, new concepts, or ideas for the participants to wrap their heads around. They provide the listener with an experience. The more you can take your listener through an experiential journey, the more successful your course will be, and the bigger the transformation for the participant.

When your participant views the presentation visuals, it is supposed to draw the learner into the experience. Enhancements pull the listener into the concepts and the flow. Enhancements will make the participant's learning memorable and effective because it's having them do some work, it's having them understand the concepts, and it solidifies the learning. As you're writing your script and developing your presentation, you need to think about where you can add enhancements. As you're moving through the scriptwriting and you're creating your presentations, you want to say, "Oh, wait, this would be a great spot for an enhancement," or "What might the enhancement look like?"

Sprinkling enhancements throughout your course will elevate the structure. Using the enhancements before, during, or after the lessons will wow the participants and increase the value of your course.

You can deliver course enhancements during the course, such as polling or a call to action. A precourse enhancement might be adding a short video at the beginning or start of every module or at the groupings of lessons. You can set it up so the participant can pause a lesson to take any action in the middle of a class or a real-time quiz that validates the learning before moving on. They can complete an exercise, complete worksheets, use downloadable resources, view a progression bar that helps the participant monitor their progress, or even issue a certificate of completion. Then there's after the course.

Remember adding enhancements will increase the experience. Depending on how many enhancements you create and what you're offering, it can increase the value of your course.

The best way to decide where to integrate the enhancements into your course is to ask yourself, "What is it that my listeners want?" Keep in mind what you wanted the learner to learn and what you wanted the learners to do after the course. It's really about the transformation you want them to have.

Downloads. The most common enhancement course creators offer at the end of modules or lessons is a downloadable document. It just seems to be what and where people are comfortable adding enhancements. Downloadable documents allow participants to take action at the end of the course, end of a module, or after each lesson. That's what we're going for, for them to act. Therefore, it deserves a special callout here.

Course creators offer downloadable documents and usually convert them into PDF format. A PDF seems to be the most common method for most people to download a copy easily, and the course creator can easily convert a document into a PDF format.

When we create downloadable documents at the end of each lesson, we feel there is an immediacy to acting, and the learner can say, "I'm going to do it now" or "I'm going to take action." This is what's important—for people to take action toward their transformation.

There are a variety of different types of downloads you can offer. There are action or activity sheets, workbooks, or worksheets. You can name the download what you wish. Sometimes people like the term action sheets; some people like the term coursework sheets. It is important to name it to match your brand, what your avatar likes, and whatever makes sense within your program. If you don't want to do an activity sheet or worksheet, you can create lists or check sheets. Everybody loves check sheets, check, check, check, check!

You can create samples, such as a sample letter. You can offer templates. For example, if you're teaching presentation skills, you could give a sample presentation template. Resource sheets are great. We like resource sheets. We think resource sheets allow people to take away one sheet that they can go to and say, "Oh yeah, I needed this, and now I can refer to it easily." We've also done resource sheets about books or articles to read. It doesn't have to be a resource sheet with just links or something you're referring to, but you can create resource sheets based on things you want them to learn or additional thought-provoking opportunities.

It's best to explore what type of downloads you may want to create and what your listeners will want and need.

Storyboard. Often fiction writers use storyboards to help develop their storylines and character development. Storyboards are used in the entertainment industry to help create the storyline for the film. We advocate creating a course storyboard to help develop a picture of what your course will look like and how it will flow. Storyboards allow you to build your script and match it to your visuals.

Storytelling. The power of storytelling is magical. Stories are what people love to hear. People will connect with you if you can tell a story with authenticity, entertainment, and a message. When they connect with you, they connect with the material; when people connect with the material, they are more likely to act and have the desired results your course promises.

Production Schedule

Creating a production schedule will keep you accountable for the launch date goal you wrote down when you created your course plan. A production schedule and timeline should include start dates and finish dates. A production schedule includes:

- start dates and completion dates
- discovery processes and brainstorming sessions
- business plan development
- scalability model outline and content
- script development
- enhancement development
- download development
- production outline
- recordings: videotaping and voice-over
- editing
- PowerPoints (to be converted into the video)
- Learning Management System selection and landing page
- upload to the platform
- launch and marketing

When it comes to creating your production schedule, please take the time to make a robust schedule. If you complete it thoughtfully with realistic expectations, you could have your course completed within three months—without it, you will probably be talking about creating your course for the next year or more.

Wow. We know that was a lot for one chapter, but now you can work on creating your script that will make your course worth your time and your client's time. As a recap, we covered scripting: the importance of timing, language, clarity, questions, time stamping, infotainment, visuals, enhancements, storyboards, and storytelling. And we talked about the importance of and what should be included in developing your production schedule.

Up next is production. In the following chapter, you will learn tips and tricks for producing your course, recording your video and audio, how to record voice-overs, and editing your content.

Take Action

What type of enhancements will you include in your digital product?

What type of downloads will you include in your digital product?

Create your production schedule.

Start to create your storyboard.

CHAPTER 8

Production: Ideation, Planning, And Execution

Create your own visual style...Let it be unique
for yourself and yet identifiable to others.
ORSON WELLES

HERE WE ARE. You have written your script, identified enhancements, and outlined your downloads. You should feel excited and accomplished. It's time to implement your production schedule.

As we work through this chapter, the intent is to share tips and tricks so you can be more confident and produce your course like a pro. Production is about formatting your course for client value, meeting your avatar's desires and likes, creating amazing videos and voice-overs, and editing.

Presentation Style

When deciding which style to use to present your course, there are two factors to consider: you, as the instructor, and your client, as the avatar. Both play an equally significant role in production.

Avatar. Revisit the avatar you identified earlier in Chapter 3. Remember to speak to one specific person and then create your product to help one person solve a problem and transform. Having an in-depth understanding of your avatar will help you navigate some of the production questions you may have as you start to produce your course. To help, here are a few additional questions you should ask yourself:

- What are the avatar's preferred learning styles?

- How do they prefer to receive information?

- Do they like to see topics reinforced after the discussion?

- Do they like a speech-style presentation?

- Perhaps a quick lesson followed by bullet points, a quiz, or an assessment to check their understanding of the content presented?

- Would they like a how-to video or a demonstration of how to accomplish something?

- What appeals visually to your avatar to keep them infotained?

- Videos, pictures, slide decks, cartoons, or lists?

- What visuals will appeal to your avatar?

- Do they like conservative visuals or off-the-hook wild?

When producing your course, you must study your avatar. If you are still at a loss, an excellent way to gain clarity regarding your avatar is to interview people who would benefit from your course. You will get the exact information you need to get your message across on your visuals.

Presentation Format

The following are various options to consider when you begin to produce your course:

Voice-over. How will you present your course? You can create different visual styles. One would be a slide deck with you recording your voice or hiring a professional voice-over artist. There is an all-video presentation or mixed media with a hybrid of slides and videos. The hybrid model is our preferred method for our clients. Which presentation style is best for you? Where are you most comfortable—in front of the camera or out of the camera view? If you are a bit shy, producing a slide deck with a voice-over could be for you. If you are not comfortable on camera, if you want to read a script from notes and not spend a lot of time memorizing the script, then voice-over is probably the best option.

If your audience prefers to follow the content as you speak, if you want an easy way to produce the course with less time, and if you don't present well, you can always hire a voice-over artist to do the audio.

A disadvantage of producing a slide deck with only voice-over is that it can lack the instructor's personality and the participant may feel disconnected. If you choose this style, then be sure your graphics are well done and you have exciting animation.

Video. Do your participants want a personal connection with you? Does your participant wish to see your excitement or emotion as you present your content? Are you experienced onstage presenting keynotes? Then you may be comfortable filming your content and delivering it in an all-video format.

Keep in mind that delivering a speech in front of an audience is not the same as when you film, where you won't have the crowd's energy. A benefit of video is that you have many styles and options: different scenes, setups, and presentation enhancements.

What is your experience on camera? There are some factors to consider when filming your content—plan to rehearse more when doing video than if you did an all-slide voice-over production. The production time will be longer, as it takes more time to video record than a voice-over, and it is more intense during the editing process. If you choose to use a professional studio for filming, production will be more expensive. The good news is that there are many choices for filming that are less expensive than a full day at the studio. There are webcams, computers, and cell phones and they are all options that do a pretty dang good job. We'll discuss equipment and the how-to later in the chapter.

Video And Voice-over. By combining video and voice-over in a hybrid product and mixing in the media, you can have the best of both worlds. The participant can connect with you because you produce a product that allows your participants to follow along with slide visuals mixed in, or you can overlay them on top of your video. Depending on the number of slides and video mix, it's easier to produce than an all-video.

You may need to be more tech-savvy for an all-video production. There is an increased cost, and it takes more time to produce the finished videos. The number of animations, overlays, or other video enhancements determines the cost and time involved. In most cases, producing a mixed-media product versus an all-voice-over product requires a higher degree of sophistication. But again, there are many options to help you create a hybrid product. To name one, you can use casting platforms such as Zoom to record.

Which presentation style is best for you? There is no universal right or wrong or better or best way to present. Pick a style that works for you as the instructor and a style that works for your avatar. Some well-known course creators began behind a slide presentation and then grew to move in front of the camera. Do what's best for you. We will share tips, tricks, and resources to help you produce a product like a pro.

Video And Audio Tips And Tricks

Here are some voice-over tips and tricks:

- *Your position while speaking.* Do you want to sit or stand? Our preferred method is standing. Standing tends to give you stronger vocals when you are speaking.

- *The microphone placement.* If you are using a standing mic, place your mic approximately six inches from your mouth to capture your voice just right. If the microphone is too far away, you'll sound echoey—too close, you'll sound breathy.

- *Script placement.* Place your script at eye level so your stature is upright, and your projection is forward. You don't want to be looking down.

- *Recording location.* Beware of rigid objects next to you. Hard surfaces cause the sound to bounce back. So how do you fix the sound from bouncing? You taped your script to the wall, and you are now recording facing that wall.

You can pin a towel or some fabric to absorb the sound waves. This idea may seem funny, but even going into your closet to record can make a great sound studio.

- *Recording levels.* Make sure you're testing. Test that you are not too loud or too quiet and that the sound levels are consistent throughout your course.

When recording a voice-over, here are some tips for preparing yourself to do a great job:

- *Script.* Mark up your script where you will pause and emphasize where you're going to take a breath. Make a note of where you will inflect up or down at the end of the sentence to emphasize the information.

- *Rehearse.* The professionals say you should rehearse a script at least ten times before recording.

- *Water.* Be hydrated before you start and have a glass next to you to soothe your throat throughout the entire recording.

- *Exercise.* There are two types of exercises: physical activity for your body and exercising your vocals. Physical exercise gets your blood flowing, so jump, stretch, wind up, dance—get your energy up. Your vocals need to be warmed up. Sing lalalalala, ooh eeh ooh aah, ooh eeh ooh aah, and red leather, yellow leather, red leather, yellow leather ten times. Now, you are ready to press the record button.

During the recording, here are some things to consider:

- *Your personality.* Be yourself. Don't get caught up in the process.

- *Pace.* Watch your pace. Don't go too fast, or your listeners will have to keep rewinding to hear your message. Too slow of a pace and your listeners will lose interest.

- *Diction and pronunciation.* Use language related to your avatar and words and phrases you are familiar with and can pronounce.

- *Breathing.* Use natural breathing during the recording, as you have marked up in your script for those breaths. These tips are the same ones that professionals use. Go record like a pro.

Here are some camera tips and tricks:

- *Cameras.* There are various types of cameras: your computer, your phone, or a digital camera. The camera on your computer is not as good as a phone, but you could upgrade to a webcam for better quality if you choose to use your computer. Your iPhone can be as good as an expensive digital camera. When using your iPhone, you want to make sure you use the lens on the back of your phone. Don't do selfie-style filming, although it is easier to see yourself in the frame.

- *Camera placement.* Use a tripod or stable surface to secure your camera or phone. When using your phone, the phone must be horizontal, not vertical.

We will now discuss several tips and tricks for filming.

Lighting. Lots of people ask if they need to invest in lighting. If you are interested in purchasing lighting, you might want to look at a ring light or box light. But there are household options that could do the trick too. If you choose to use household lighting, use a desk or table lamp without the shade. Depending on the light bulbs' lumens and warmth or coolness, the overhead light might be a good option. Whether purchasing lighting or selecting the home option, use multiple lights. Place the lighting at various levels to eliminate any shadowing, which means some lights may be on the floor or behind you. Also, the use of natural lighting is the best.

Green screen versus a staged studio set has become a common conversation. Green screens are inexpensive and often easy to put up. If you go with the green screen option, you must light both the green screen and you. It isn't easy to correctly light a green screen; it takes a lot of testing. When using a green screen, you should stand at least four to six feet away from the screen for the best results. If you choose to use a virtual background (like the ones on Zoom), you must use a green screen behind you. Without the green screen, you end up with the ghosting of your body parts.

If you choose to create a staged set in your home or office, make sure it represents your brand and shows your authority on the subject matter. When you stage your space, ensure it is not cluttered, and know what's behind you. We have witnessed the dual space showing laundry or empty drink bottles from the party the night before. Do your best to angle yourself so you have nothing poking out of your head or body. People expect a well-lighted, staged, and branded background with no ghosting.

Rule of Thirds. Let's check your placement in the frame with the rule of thirds. You should be placed slightly off-center at about one-third to the side, and your eyes should be about at the one-third level as shown.

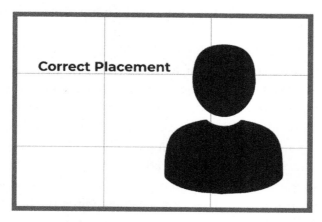

If you have an iPhone, go to your camera settings, and turn on the "view grid." If you don't have the capability of a grid, be aware of how the rule of thirds works from these examples.

When in the correct position, you will fill up the frame and it looks great. When sitting in the frame, you should not be looking up or down at the participants. It would be best if you were level with them. Think of it like this: do you look like you are having a conversation at Starbucks across the table? If the answer is yes, then you have good placement. Here is a tip about Zoom: when recording, look at the green camera light, not the participants. If you tell a critical story or record a video sales letter, your placement should be in the middle of the frame. Keep in mind, your eyes should still use the rule of thirds.

When setting up, you found it takes time to set up your equipment properly. You got it perfect, don't lose it; mark your setup with painter-type removable tape. Mark your microphones, your lights, your tripod, where you put the camera, and the place you were standing or sitting. Marking the spots will save you time in the future and keep your videos consistent.

Equipment. Equipment can significantly range in price. Here are some equipment options you may need to purchase: a webcam, lighting, microphones, or items for your staged setting.

There are many types of webcams you can attach to your computer. Webcams can cost about fifty bucks to several hundred dollars. You can purchase other types of cameras, but they will be more expensive. When using your camera or cell phone, you may also need to invest in additional accessories, such as a tripod, a smartphone adapter, or a lens enhancer.

Lighting can cost from twenty-five to hundreds of dollars. Tripods can run you about thirty dollars. Often the best value is purchasing packages that include accessories.

There is a range of microphones, and they vary in price points. The Blue Yeti is expected to cost about two hundred dollars, and the podcast kit runs approximately one hundred dollars or more. If you are standing and filming with your cell phone, you will need a quality microphone with at least a six-foot cord. Do not use the mike on your phone as the sound will not be clear and crisp.

The next section will cover slide creation, conversion to videos, adding audio to your presentation, and editing.

Creating Slides. For the ease of creating your slide presentation, a few software options can help you, even for the creatively challenged. Most people are familiar with PowerPoint presentations. PowerPoint is usually standard software already installed on your PC and Keynote on a Mac. Both options have templates that you can begin with and then trade out the content, pictures, and branding colors and make them your own. If you are unfamiliar with automation, such as text floating or fade-in and fade-outs, you might need some assistance. It is very easy to time your slides and record your voice-overs directly in PowerPoint. Once you have completed your PowerPoint, simply go to the dropdown and save it as an MP4. You can record your audio directly into the latest version of PowerPoint. Or you can find recording software, record your audio, and then edit it into your PowerPoint. If you are going to record video, you can use a camera or your phone and then insert the video into your PowerPoint video via editing software.

Another hot product right now is Canva. If you are unfamiliar with Canva, it's like having your own design studio. There are so many templates to choose from, including stock photos and videos. Even the creatively challenged can produce beautiful projects. Currently, there are options to record video and audio directly into your project from Canva. The video will be small, so this might not be a good option if you are trying to be on camera while telling an impactful story.

Next is PresenterMedia, although there is other similar software that you can buy. Once you have seen the presentations you can make in PresenterMedia, you may never use PowerPoint again. The template animation that PresenterMedia provides in their slides allows even the novice to produce a professional animated presentation. You can record directly in Canva with or without showing your face or another option is to record your presentation in Zoom. When we produce clients digital products, we use multiple software programs that require experience and expertise. But for the do-it-yourselfers, there are many options as mentioned above.

Editing. You've done your slides, your audio, and video, and now it's time to edit. The purpose of editing is to create the wow factor. You can improve most videos by adding extra elements. During editing, you can eliminate bangs or loud breaths in your voice-over. Editing corrects the timing of your slides, and some minor flaws in your recording to make you sound great. Adding some music will enhance the viewing experience, just like the background music in a movie enhances the scene.

Here are some editing software options: you can use Movie Maker if you operate a PC or iMovie if you are using a Mac. You could purchase a Camtasia license if you are ready to go pro and have great enhancements to your video, such as quiz replay, or allowing participants to choose their own path and journey through your course. We use all the above plus Adobe. Adobe allows us to produce videos offering a movie-like production.

Gathering all the elements and incorporating them into a finished product can be challenging, especially if you are not a creative or a techie person. Before recording and spending a lot of time on your project:

1. Consider your skills. If you need someone to edit, you should bring that person on to your team way before you begin to do any recording.

2. Get your storyboard done before you do any recording.

3. Set up your studio and complete a sound check before recording.

4. And then practice, practice, practice.

We have received calls from people who are super excited they have recorded all their videos—that's a lot of time and effort. But when the editing process begins, it becomes apparent to the editor that the sound is terrible, the body placement is bad, the scripting isn't broken down correctly, and it is impossible to make cuts in the video or audio. Don't be that person; get your team together early before you put in the effort of recording a video or your audio. This is where going slow at first will pay off big. You will be well prepared for when you go into your home studio or a professional studio.

We have mentioned many options. Technology and equipment are constantly changing, and you should do your due diligence before purchasing. Do your research and decide on the equipment or software that fits your budget. Remember, production is about creating entertaining visuals, good lighting, and great-sounding audio. If you've done this, you will have created a successful digital product.

Next up, we will discuss technology.

Take Action

What presentation format will you choose?

- voice-over

- video only

- hybrid of voice-over and video

What do you need to purchase to get started?

CHAPTER 9

Decrypting Technology Complexities

Embrace technology; don't become it.
GERD LEONHARD, FUTURIST AND HUMANIST

YOU HAVE CREATED your course, and now the question is, where do you make it available for purchase? Understanding technology is another stage in course creation that may get a bit perplexing. But don't worry; we will uncover several options for you.

The three specific ways to operate and sell your course are through: your website, a marketplace, and a Learning Management System. We will highlight these choices and the different functionalities so you can choose the one that best fits you and your client's needs.

Website. One option is for your customer to visit your current website and click on an action button that sends them to the LMS platform you have selected. Or your webmaster can construct an integrated e-commerce site and a back-end method to deliver the course to your clients—the latter is more expensive.

Using your website, you can find a plug-in where the advantages are less like a template that has few customizable options. Using a plug-in gets more complicated to implement, so you will need some tech know-how. You'll also need to find a video hosting platform like Vimeo or YouTube to make it functional.

Marketplace. An online marketplace is an e-commerce website where multiple third parties provide products and services. Sometimes people think a marketplace sounds like a good idea because all the marketing is done for you; they run promotions, you have a large audience, and it's a low-risk investment. That sounds great, right? However, people don't identify with your brand when using a marketplace. It may not be your target audience. You have no control over the pricing, as they can run a promotion at any time at any price. They lock you into their format with no control over design and function. It is wise to consider these issues if you want to operate in a marketplace. If it works for your business model, then go for it.

Learning Management Systems. What is an LMS platform? It's simply a software application that will help you operate your eLearning business. It provides automation that replaces rigorous and expensive manual work, saves time, and enables you to organize your content and data. It tracks and reports on training activity and results for each learner. It helps organizations manage training events, self-paced courses, and blended learning programs. Some features are collecting payment from your customer, administrative tasks, documentation, tracking the users for follow-up, progress reporting, and developing and hosting your eLearning course.

Here are the things to consider when choosing an LMS platform.

Ease of use. Are you more techie, or do you lack tech experience? Some are easier to use than others. How are you delivering the content, including the enhancements? Does the price fit your budget, and are you limited by the number of users or courses? Can you drip the delivery of content on a schedule? Is video hosting included, or will you need a third-party video hosting provider?

Do you need marketing support, such as prebuilt sales pipelines or funnels? Do they support the enhancements you want to offer in your course? Do you need it to integrate with other systems? Are you interested in gamification, such as badges or points? Do you want the users to see a progress bar? Would you like an affiliate sales option where other people sell your course for a percentage of the sales? And make sure your course can be seen on a tablet or mobile device. As you can see, there are many features that LMS platforms can provide.

Think about the course experience you want your participants to have well before getting overwhelmed and confused about which platform to choose. For this book's printing, here are some of the most popular platforms: Kajabi, Thinkific, Teachable, Podia, Kartra, and our all-in-one KMS Powered platform.

Kajabi is one of many platforms with brand recognition. It can replace a few other applications in your business, such as your website, an e-commerce site, and your customer relationship management (CRM). It has prebuilt email marketing campaigns. You can run a membership site out of Kajabi. It has easy, beautiful, and somewhat customizable templates, but it is one of the most expensive platforms. However, the cost may not be a factor if it is right for you and can replace other applications in your business.

With Thinkific, it has fast load times and good customization, delivers a great user experience, and you can bundle your courses. Teachable's primary focus is on courses. This may be a good platform for you if you are technically challenged. Teachable has limited customization, but it's easy to use. One of the great features of Teachable is that you can translate your course into other languages; they hold your funds for thirty days.

Next is Podia, which has instant payouts. You can integrate your blog, and if you're already on a platform, their customer service can help you transfer a course. The attractive price points of Podia, Teachable, and Thinkific are all similar.

Kartra is like Kajabi—it is a good platform also with brand recognition. It is another platform with plenty of predesigned campaigns, an added calendar, help desk, and support tickets for your customers to send to you. And if you have a product like a book, you can sell it from the Kartra site. Kartra is a little more difficult to use than Kajabi, but there is a price difference.

KMS Powered is an all-in-one integrated system for coaches and consultants. (www.KMSPowered.com)

An integrated system is a holistic approach to running a business without the hassle of using an assortment of technology platforms. Leveraging KMS Powered automation capabilities will help a business owner scale and will give them time back in their day to focus on the important work—serving clients.

KMS Powered lets coaches and consultants systematize:

- Digital product offerings such as eCourses and academies

- Coaching and consulting package offers and purchases

- Processes and systematize tasks that are necessary but repetitive

- Customer Services Management (CRM) is integrated

- eCommerce, creating and sending proposals, invoicing, and sales tracking

- Marketing campaign management including funnels

- Scheduling client meetings and sessions

- Text and email notifications

- Integration of new landing pages for a website (or eliminate the need for a website)

- Licensing and certifications of a framework

- And much more...

KMS Powered is easy to use and has plenty of templates. Business owners can set it up themselves, or they can hire someone like us to set up the business systems and automations. The integrated system can be set up with a few products and automations at first, and as the company grows, the system grows.

KMS Powered is priced extremely competitively because we want to help business owners avoid the chaos of managing multiple piecemeal software programs, easily scale their business, and have time to do their best work.

We offer KMS Powered as a standalone system, or we help clients put all the pieces together to integrate their business. As a personal note, we operate our business through KMS Powered.

A new platform is created every day, and prices are constantly changing, so do your due diligence. The critical point here is knowing what you want your course to offer the learner, what you want a client to experience, and your technical capabilities. Then you can choose the right operating system for you.

Take Action

What type of platform will you select? And why?

- Website—Why?

- Marketplace—Why?

- Learning Management System—Why?

What can you automate and systematize to help scale your business?

If you have any questions about what was covered in this chapter, please reach out to us at Kaleidoscopemediaservices.com. For more on the technology platform, visit: KMSPowered.com

Part III

*And if the end result is that someone,
somewhere winds up believing they
can do something out of the ordinary,
well, then you've really made it.*

ANGELA AHRENDTS, FORMER HEAD
OF APPLE'S RETAIL DIVISION

CHAPTER 10

The Launch Code

Success requires three bones–wishbone, backbone, and funny bone.
REBA MCENTIRE, FEMALE RECORDING ARTIST, ACTOR, & BUSINESSWOMAN

REGISTRATION IS OPEN. Here we are, the most exciting time in your course creation journey. After weeks or months of hard work developing your course, the time has finally arrived to launch.

It's Not A Secret

Hey, guess what? Your course is not a secret. Start talking about it. Share what you are developing to spark buyers' interest in potential purchases. If your course is still in development, get input. This prelaunch stage is no time to be silent. First, educate. You did not build your course to keep it a secret. Start shouting it out. Tell people what you are doing and what your course is offering. Build some excitement around it. Share the results your course will deliver.

Campaign

What do you do? After building your email list, it's time to send the prospect through an automated marketing campaign. These campaigns are built with planned content released in a timed sequence called a drip script. A simple five-sequence campaign:

> Email 1: To introduce you as an expert, introduce your course, and get them engaged and interested.
>
> Email 2: To share the insights of your course.
>
> Email 3: To review the solution you are solving and why they need your course.
>
> Email 4: To address any objections the buyer may have.
>
> Email 5: This is your final pitch to the buyer on why they should buy your course.

Keep in mind when building your email series, your "call to action" or the "buy button" should be in every email. Different buyers will buy at different times in the sequence.

Video Sales Letter

A video sales letter is a modern version of a traditional sales letter. In this age of video communication, smartphones, and short attention spans, the average person is less inclined to read, especially if the content is trying to sell them something. When creating a video sales letter, you should make it short, just a couple of minutes. It should immediately engage the viewer so they will watch it until the end. And the call to action should be prominent. Give them access to the buy link immediately. Make it easy to click the button, "buy my course."

Don't send them away to your website to find a button to buy your course.

Here is the perfect video sales letter formula:

- Get their attention, and shock and surprise them.

- Identify the problem and not only identify the problem, but also agitate it a bit.

- Explain the solution.

- Now's the time to introduce the product or service.

- What results will they get or benefits from doing business with you?

Then the next two are interchangeable:

- You can do a call to action first, followed by social proof, or start with social proof and then a call to action. Social proof can be a testimonial, a case study, or statistics.

- If you are new and do not have any case studies or testimonials, pull some statistics off the internet to support the purchase.

- Lastly, as an option, you can throw in a bonus at the end of your video sales letter.

Launching Your Course

There are two registration methods: the launch and the evergreen process. The big difference between the two is that a live launch tends to generate more revenue in a short period, while an evergreen model produces a steady stream of income. The secret is to understand your audience and have an awareness of their preferences.

Launch. If you choose the launch process, here are some things to consider. Your registration is not always available for purchase. You select only specific periods of the year to promote and sell your course. The timing could be quarterly, twice a year, or once a year. The launch method can have you on a revenue roller coaster—money in, then no money, then money in, and then no money. But it also creates a sense of urgency to buy now.

Evergreen. With the evergreen process, you will market your course with regular marketing activities like your business. Your course registration is always open for purchase. You may have one or multiple courses to sell on the same site. This method is an opportunity to build a reoccurring revenue stream, helps create stability, and allows you to scale your business.

When choosing the launch or evergreen method, understanding each process is good. But each method has different marketing activities. They each have specific outcomes. Choose the one that aligns with your business model.

Upsells

An upsell is when you try to convince a customer to purchase something additional or at a higher price.

We experience upsells when we purchase from Amazon. You have seen the advertisements: "Customers who have bought this have also purchased this," when you are shopping on Amazon's site.

It is an excellent idea to develop, or at least know, what upsell packages you will offer before you complete your course. Upsells could include your coaching or consulting packages, masterminds, or workshops, to name a few. To help you with the upsell package development, refer to the flywheel, scalability model, and business plan that you worked on during Chapters 2 and 4.

Bundles

Bundle pricing is a method of selling a set of items as a package for a price lower than the items would cost if sold separately. Think of it like purchasing a value meal at a fast-food restaurant. Imagine you offer three different courses at ninety-nine dollars each. You could bundle and sell all three for $199. And just like that, by offering bundles, you instantly doubled your sales by convincing the customer to buy all three courses instead of one.

Affiliate Sales

You may want to consider affiliate sales. Affiliate sales are a method in which one company may affiliate with another company to sell its products or services. For example, fitness instructors may want to affiliate with nutritionists to sell nutritional courses to their clients and receive a commission on each sale. The great thing about an affiliate program is increasing your sales without any marketing efforts. With affiliate programs, people you don't even know can sell your course.

Licensing

An option is to license a course to others or license the use of a proven framework. Licensing can be a lucrative option for authors, speakers, coaches, and consultants who want to scale their business in a bigger, bolder way and transform more lives with their message. April, one of our clients, licensed her course for a fifty-fifty revenue split with an up-front fee of $4,500 to use the material for one year. This is just one model; there are many models for licensing your work that we have found to be successful. We created our Systematic Product and Services Licensing Program to help those who are interested in accelerated growth and want to generate a new type of revenue stream.

No matter your plan, you may choose to hire a marketing person specializing in eLearning course launches.

But whether you hire someone to help you or do it yourself, as you plan your campaign or types of sales, make sure you return to your scalability model and business plan. Knowing your business model, strategy, purpose, ideal avatar, and desired outcomes, you are on your way to making your sales goals.

Take Action

Identify what launch method works best for your business.

What upsell package will you offer?

What type of bundles will you offer?

Identify your prospective affiliates.

Ask yourself if licensing your work is an option.

CHAPTER 11

Amplifying Your Reach

Stick to your true north—build
greatness for the long term.
RUTH PORAT, CFO OF ALPHABET INC.

CONGRATULATIONS—YOU ACCOMPLISHED YOUR goal and created an eLearning course. But what's next in scaling your business? In this chapter, we solve the question of how to engage your customer after the sale. Other resources will help you with your business model continuum now that you have moved into the digital world.

What's Next For Your Client Engagement?

What should you do after someone purchases your course?

We encourage you to continue to engage your list. Yes, this is your list of buyers and nonbuyers. It is important to stay relevant to your list of contacts. The goal is for the person on your list to remember you as the expert on your subject. You may want to offer additional services or products that enhance the content of your course. Another way to stay engaged is by hosting small virtual events or prerecorded microcourses with free or paid registrations. You can share updates on what you are doing in your field to stay current. Share the new courses and other types of business services you offer. A great way to provide value is to share articles and news on your subject.

Promote. It is important to keep in contact with those who purchased your course for various reasons. But two key reasons: testimonials and promotion. We recommend you contact clients and ask for a course testimonial so you can use them on your social media feeds. Another way is to promote and highlight your customers' successes and transformations to reinforce you are the subject matter expert.

Lifetime Customers. The strategy here is to regularly deliver value and keep you top of mind with your customer. You turn your buyers into lifetime customers when continuing to deliver value. When someone is a lifetime customer, they feel at ease coming back to you for additional services. The financial advantage of building a lifetime customer is you don't have to spend new dollars on client acquisition. Therefore, you can easily offer the client your premium high-ticket package.

Referrals. When customers reach the outcome they desire, and you continue to deliver value, this builds a referral path. Again, you don't have to spend new dollars on client acquisition. Plus, the person referred comes to you with a higher level of trust than a cold lead.

Next Level. Have you considered selling your courses at the next level? Introducing your course to companies and organizations for multiple sales? You can do this through bundling packages, open monthly access, or a flat-fee licensing option.

What's Next For Your Business?

In the next few paragraphs, we will share additional strategies to consider as you scale your business now that you know how to create and add a digital product. We asked our trusted advisors, vendors, and strategic partners to provide a quick note about the importance of each strategy.

Social Media/Influencer. Sarah Olea, founder Identity Amplified.

Why Is Social Media Important?

"TV and radio were once influential. Now, social media possesses more influential power. Businesses grow their reach using social media. What used to cost millions for companies now costs thousands. Businesses that can't invest still see increasing reach by posting meaningful content directly to their target audience." Social media is essential.

Funnels. Jennifer Tamborski, founder Virtual Marketing Expert.

Why Are Funnels Important?

"Think about how much easier it is to build trust with potential clients when you use a sales funnel. Your automated process will ensure that all of those people go through an introduction, evaluation stage and conversion until they become loyal customers! This means more revenue for yourself as well increased scalability."

Networking. Kelli Holmes, founder & CEO TEAM Referral Network.

Why Is Networking Important?

"It expands our business base. We must be continually adding to our prospects and connections. We need a constant source of new business possibilities to increase our opportunities! Effective

Networking can be a way of life and is one of the most powerful techniques you can master to succeed!"

Brand Photos. Starla Fortunato, Starla Fortunato a Luxury Content photographer & producer.

Why Are Brand Photos Important?

"You have three seconds to capture someone's attention, in our digital world text alone fades away without a photo to help tell your brand's story. Well-crafted images share your business, service and products in an instant without saying a word."

Personal Branding. Sybil Henry, founder The Style Concierge.

Why Is Personal Brand Important?

"Your personal brand represents you, your deepest inner self, expressed outwardly as the visual, verbal, and experiential embodiment of how you show up. Your audience forms an opinion from their impression and perception about who they think you are. Your personal brand attracts most abundantly when it accurately reflects you."

Speaking Presence. Arvee Robinson, founder Arvee Robinson International.

Why Is Speaking Presence Important?

"Public speaking is imperative to amplify your reach and only you can do it. That's right, you have a message to share that only you can share to people that can only hear it from you. If you don't amplify your own unique message than it will be unspoken forever."

Speaking Gigs. Leisa Reid, founder Get Speaking Gigs Now.

Why Is Public Speaking Important?

"Public speaking is a quick business growth strategy! Many entrepreneurs get stuck before getting started because they don't know how to get booked or how to monetize speaking. Speaking gives you credibility and visibility."

Video Presence. Patrick McGowan, founder of Punchn.

Why Is Video Presence Important?

"Video is how we do business now. It's a video-first market and how you show up says a lot about you. Those who learn to master this new medium will have the advantage. You can be just as influential on camera as you are in person."

Publishing. Henry DeVries, founder & CEO Indie Books International.

Why Is Publishing A Book Important?

"A published book positions you as an expert, grows your business, opens up opportunities to get on more stages, and you will make a bigger impact."

Indie Books International is our publisher. The company is a hybrid between traditional publishing and self-publishing. The team helps you get your hardback, paperback, or ebook out to your audience in a professional and timely manner. They walk you through the entire book-writing process, publish your book, and teach you how to market it. Henry DeVries, CEO, has created a systematic approach that makes writing your book easy and doable. If you contact Indie Books International, you will become part of a community of authors like none other.

As a Course Creator, you can now take the content you created, expand on it, and write the book you have always wanted to write.

When you choose to reach out to any one of the people mentioned, please mention us so they know you are serious about working with them. We choose to work with people who are highly qualified and sought after for their expertise. We give each of them a shout-out for their generosity in allowing us to add them to our book.

As you build your business, it is important to do your due diligence when selecting the advisors who are right for your situation and business. We have many other connections and work with other stellar people—we just couldn't fit them all into this book. If you are looking for us to help you with your eCourse, online community, membership site, automating your systems, or you would like the names of some of our other trusted advisors, please contact us.

With that said, no matter what, remember it is important you build a team to help you create a scalable, salable, and successful product.

Take Action

Who do you need to talk with to help you create your digital product and amplify your reach?

Write down who you need on your team to help you create your digital product.

CHAPTER 12

Staying Confident
And Connected

*Timing, perseverance, and ten years of trying will
eventually make you look like an overnight success.*
BIZ STONE, COFOUNDER OF TWITTER

WELL, HERE WE are—at the end of the book but not at the
end of your journey. Let's review.

You eliminated the consulting and coaching breaking point
on the flywheel and created your new business model adding
a digital product.

You learned how to outline and write your course so you
can take your participants on a transformational journey. You
learned about scripting, components, consistency, and timing
for your course.

You have tools to build and produce an eye-catching presentation that engages and wows. And you decided how you
would build your course as a voice-over only or hybrid.

You gained knowledge on the importance of marketing
activities before, during, and after your course. Remember your
course isn't a secret!

You are turning your buyers into lifetime customers by delivering ongoing value.

You know how to leverage your digital products. You discovered ways to sell your premium packages at the end of your courses. It is important you identify if you are using your digital product as a revenue or lead generator, and if you are using affiliates or licensing.

You discovered the selection of a Learning Management System should be completed after you plan your course, know your service offerings, and understand your entire business processes to holistically leverage technology to scale your business.

If your customer has reached the outcome they desired from you, and you continue to deliver value and remind them you are there, this will build a referral path from them to you.

You have a list of other strategies and key people to help you as you continue your path to scaling your business.

Together, all these things help you build a scalable business model by adding digital products.

It's Done! You Did It!

You have taken steps to create an eLearning course that sells and scales your business.

We want to congratulate you on your new title, "Course Creator." You now belong to an exceptional group with a collective mission to share their message, expand their reach, and serve more people.

YOUR MASTER COURSE CREATORS AND BUSINESS SCALING EXPERTS,

THERESA AND LAURA

#DREAMHIGHER

Take Action

If you need additional assistance, we are here for you.

Download resource sheets to help you with your business at www.Exposingtheelearningmystery.com.

Reach out to us and set up a discovery call at www.kaleidoscopemediaservices.com/contact and fill out the contact page. Please indicate you have read our book for special offers.

Connect with us on our socials:

> Facebook: https://www.facebook.com/ KaleidoscopeMediaServicesLLC

> LinkedIn: https://www.linkedin.com/company/ kaleidoscope-media-services/mycompany/

> Instagram: Instagram.com/ kaleidoscopemediaservices

Keep us up to date on your progress and course launch.

Please send us a note and let us know how you are digitizing yourself, automating your systems, and growing your business.

About The Authors

Theresa Ashby, PhD, MBA, COO, Kaleidoscope Media Services

Dr. Theresa M. Ashby is known as a stratologist, savvy, provocative, and genuine individual, and she is widely respected for her business acumen. Theresa is an international business and success consultant, advisor, speaker, and author passionate about driving businesses forward, which she believes helps grow the economy on all levels.

She has spent the past two decades studying what it takes to "scale your business" and is identified by Forbes.com as the business scaling expert. She is also the author of another book, *Better Implementation Now! Eight Ways Great Strategies Fail and How to Fix Them.*

She is the COO of Kaleidoscope Media Services, the host of The

Heart Hustle & Humor podcast, and serves on the board of directors for She Angels Foundation and a privately held company.

Theresa is better known as Dr. T., and she operates under the belief that giving practical, real-world, no-nonsense advice and business strategies that provide tangible results help people push through the everyday challenges of business.

She believes you must walk through life's ups and downs with courage. As a business leader, you must have the tenacity and doggedness to build your desired empire.

Her motto is, "Change the world one action at a time and have fun while doing it!"

She loves to travel and meet people on the journey, and experience the uniqueness of cultures, which expands her knowledge and appreciation of other people's thoughts and ideas.

Laura Neubauer, CEO, Kaleidoscope Media Services

Laura Neubauer is a recognized expert and serial entrepreneur. Laura Neubauer is a towering figure in the business of "scaling your business" and building self-designed business lifestyles.

The fiery entrepreneur has built and sold multiple multi-million businesses throughout her career. And has mentored other entrepreneurs through the uncertainty of the start-up phase to the growth acceleration all the way through to a successful exit. She knows first-hand how difficult it can be to build a thriving organization while managing a family.

She has been recognized as Orange County's "Entrepreneur to Watch" and California's businesswoman of the year on Forbes. com and one of Inc.'s fastest-growing companies in America.

As an influencer in the billion-dollar digital product space, Laura has helped clients leverage digital products and technology for business growth and automation. She knows how to create passion-driven business opportunities and disrupt the status quo.

Laura has spent many years on the softball field, coaching and mentoring players, where she has imparted her work ethic and values to help the next generation of youth. She has now taken this to the next level and is the master creator of ETEENPRENEUR, the leading online community that provides teen entrepreneurs with online business education and peer support. ETEENPRENEUR is built by entrepreneurs to help teens be a part of the growing entrepreneur and leadership movement.

Laura's success is based on integrity, strong relationships, and passion for seeing other people succeed.

Theresa and Laura co-founded Kaleidoscope Media Services, an internationally recognized company by the Global Federation of Education and Learning. With Theresa's and Laura's know-how, future-thinking perspective, and willingness to take a risk, they entered the digital product, technology automation, and production industry and built Kaleidoscope Media Services, a creative media agency that serves clients worldwide while earning loyal clients and followers who value their "straightforward" and "genuine" advice.